PRAISE FOR 'J.

"Jamie has a wealth of propert_____ _____ that having him in your team will propel you to success. Jamie has such an approachable manner that you are confident that you can ask him anything, even better than that you know he has the answers too!

When Jamie told me my business idea would be a success I was overjoyed, partly because that is what I needed to hear, but more importantly he is such a respected property investor that to hear it from him was something very special indeed.

When you decide you need to learn something you look for a teacher, if you are lucky enough to find Jamie then you have more than a teacher you have a business colleague, someone who invests both in property and also in you."

BARBARA BANNISTER

"I have worked with Jamie for over two years and have always been impressed with his professionalism, intelligence and passion."

TRISTAN BRAY

"Jamie's passion to help others invest in property is remarkable. He is very practical, kind and extremely helpful. Having left his corporate job to become a full time property investor, Jamie doesn't just talk the talk, but he also walks the walk. He is a pleasure to deal with."

TANYA BURCH

"Jamie has a great mentoring style: he's relaxed, experienced and very approachable. Jamie also knows how to provide the perfect combination of encouragement, education and gentle boot up the backside (I needed all three!). I now have greater confidence in my abilities, a better knowledge of the right questions to ask, and a do-able action plan for my particular property strategy. I'm out there, applying what I've learned. Thank you for your mentorship and insight, Jamie!"

VIVIANA LOTTI

"I believe that Jamie has truly added value to the beginning of my property career. He has answered my questions, shared his knowledge with me and I'd recommend him to anyone who wants to learn more about property."

STEVE MITCHELL

"I have spoken to Jamie on a number of occasions about property investing and the difficulty in taking action when trying a new investing strategy. He always managed to get to the root of the difficulty, simplify it, and suggest how to move forward and keep motivated…!"

GED MORRIS

"Jamie has always been keen to share his immense knowledge in Property Investing in a clear and concise way. As my mentor, his approach is to take away the 'noise' and to encourage me to take a simple path towards property success. As a result of his input, I am now well on my way to achieving my Property Investment Goals."

GLENN TAYLOR MNAEA, *DIRECTOR, TAYLOR GIBBS*

"I am an experienced property investor, but with the current quickly changing market I have valued the advice and suggestions Jamie has given me. His fresh pair of informed eyes on a property deal or change in strategy has helped prevent costly mistakes or a profitable opportunity missed. I wish I had had Jamie's 3PR Framework when starting out."

RACHAEL TROUGHTON

"We found Jamie very approachable, of high integrity and most of all knowledgeable about the great returns that property can offer."

GARY & JANET WEBB

"You have a wealth of knowledge and I enjoyed being mentored by you. Thanks - your advice is much appreciated."

CONRAD WOODE

The PROPERTY

IRONMAN

Health, Wealth and
Property Investment

JAMIE MADILL

This book is dedicated to my amazing wife, *Xenia*, my beautiful daughters, *Olivia & Grace*, and the rest of my family. You are the inspiration behind why I do what I do, and the reason why I am who I am.

ACKNOWLEDGMENTS

Heartfelt thanks to: Rob Moore, Mark Homer, Chrissie Wellington, Andy Harrington, Jayne Carpenter, Nick Hague, Kris Carpenter, Napoleon Hill, Bernie Murphy, Darren Hardy, Alistair and Jonny Brownlee, Sylvia & Juswant Rai, Francis Dolley, Don Fink, Maksoom Hussain, Simon Zutshi, Gill Alton, Bradley Wiggins, Steve Evans, Robert Kiyosaki, Roy Inman, Mark Cavendish, Sarah Barrett, Neil Larken, Glenn Armstrong, Jim Rohn, Johnnie Cass, Parmdeep Vadesha, Robin Shaw, James Lavers, Andy Phillips, Yvonne Emery, Paul Ribbons, Steve Watson , Julie Wright, Trevor Cutmore, Christopher Lycksell, Phil Nicholson and Daniel Wagner.

I also want to thank the hundreds of other people I have worked with, chatted to and competed against at various other property and triathlon events over the last few years. It has been fun.

CONTENTS

INTRODUCTION: INVESTING LIKE A PRO

This book is an opportunity—an opportunity to realize that you can make the money you need to thrive in this world by investing in property. But it's not your run of the mill, over-hyped, 'do this to get rich quick' book. No, no...

It's about financial freedom and the savvy process of using property investment to get it. You know where you want to be financially; you always have. For some people, it's wealthy enough to not work and to travel at least once a year. For others, it is having enough money to be able to travel any time, at any point in their lives—permanently if they like. While some others are worried that their pension will not provide for them when they stop working, and they need to take control of their retirement fund fast if they want to enjoy their later years.

Do you want any of these things?

Now, there's no getting away from the fact that it's difficult to buy property these days. Around 10 to 20 years ago it was relatively simple to buy property, and as long as you had an income and some savings, banks would lend you what you needed.

Things became even easier in the early 2000s because you often didn't need a job or any savings to get a mortgage because banks were falling over themselves to give you their cash to buy property!

Sub-prime lending and the global financial crisis changed all that, and it is now tougher than it has been in a long time to get a mortgage in many countries of the world.

When banks stop lending—economies flat-line, stagnate, or decline. This in turn leads to economic uncertainty, unemployment, and inflation, and these problems led banks to become stricter about who they lend money to, and that makes it more difficult for hard-working people such as you and me to buy property.

Similarly, when there is so much doom and gloom in the news about the economy, everyone around us suddenly becomes an expert and warns us off doing anything they think is risky.

What's worse is that everyone else's doubts infect us, and typically we start to question ourselves. The little voice in our head warns us not to take risks and to wait it out until things get better. The chances are that the more you listen to that little voice in your head, those around you or the media, the less likely it is that you'll ever get started.

Does that sound familiar?

I too listened to the naysayers for far too many years and put off the start of my property investing journey. You see, I had a great job in advertising that was relatively well-paid and I sold millions of pounds worth of advertising deals for my employers for more than 18 years.

I was proud of my career. I won some awards and that helped boost my ego, but underneath all that I still had the same frustrations as many others. I was passed over for promotion a few times, worked long hours, got caught up in a lot of office politics, and hardly ever saw Xenia, my wife, and Olivia and Grace, my children, during the week.

At weekends, I was exhausted and was no fun to be around. I lost count of how many of my children's school events I missed out on because I was always working. In short, I was a classic corporate prisoner—I was incredibly frustrated and wanted more from my life but could not leave because I had significance through my work and lots of bills to pay!

Early on in 2010 everything changed. My wife found a lump on her leg and after various tests she was diagnosed with a rare form of cancer. Xenia and I were devastated— how could a young, beautiful woman, and a mother of two, have a life-threatening disease? What had she done to deserve that? I selfishly thought, "This stuff happens to other people, not us!"

I couldn't help thinking about the worst possible outcome and if that did happen, how on earth were Olivia and Grace going to cope without their mummy? After many operations and on-going medical treatment, and a further year of worry, Xenia finally got the all clear as the doctors had successfully removed the tumour. That news had the effect of lifting a huge weight from my shoulders, and I vowed right there and then that I would make my family my number one priority.

I would find a way to replace my salary and sack my boss so I could spend more time with those that I loved (whether they liked that or not!).

I had invested in some property in 2005-2006 and had been lured by the glossy brochures and slick presentation by a company that sold 'off-plan' apartments in the UK. The discounts they offered looked amazing, and the promised rental returns were impressive.

As a novice I did not do any due diligence, I believed what the company told me—it did not take long to realise that it was all hype. Thankfully those few apartments have always been rented out to tenants because I have had good letting agents, but they will not make me any decent money for some years yet. **Key lesson**—*do your own research and don't believe the hype!*

In 2010, I met two young guys who ran a company called Progressive Property, Rob Moore and Mark Homer, and they trained wannabe property investors on how to do it yourself. After the 'off-plan' disaster, I was never going to let someone else manage my own money ever again, so I learnt all I could and started buying two and three bed houses.

Within two years I had a million pound property portfolio and had replaced my work salary. I don't write this to impress you; I'm just an average man, and I am proof that anyone can do the same thing. I have spoken to many other property millionaires and will share some of their stories later in the book, people such as Gill Alton who is a busy mum with a property portfolio worth more than £1.6m, Neil Larken who only took three years to build a portfolio worth more than £3.6m, and Simon Zutschi whose portfolio is valued at £6m AND who has more than £7,000 per month in passive income.

The Property Ironman will teach you what it really takes to achieve this level of success. Two things define me as a person. I'm a successful property investor and a fully-fledged Ironman triathlete.

I've discovered that the two complement each other in a lot of ways. A lot of the mettle that makes me a great triathlete also makes me a great property investor. I learned to invest like a pro by applying the lessons I learned in my Ironman training.

Both disciplines take careful research, planning, and strategy. You have to follow a specific pattern, or predetermined plan, in order to succeed.

Finally, determination and action are the final weapons in your Ironman arsenal.

The reason I have based my property investment book on my Ironman training is this: *like investment, training for a triathlon is a long and gruelling process.* There is no quick and easy way to become a property magnate overnight! It just does not happen, especially in today's unstable economic climate.

An Ironman triathlon is a long-distance race run by the World Triathlon Corporation that started in Hawaii in 1978 and has now spread in popularity across the world. Other organisations hold races of the same distance, and these are 'Full Distance Triathlons'.

Ironman races are either for newbies who don't know any better, or for insane athletes who just do not feel any pain! Each race involves swimming for 3.86 kilometres, cycling for 180 kilometres, and running 42.2 kilometres— all without stopping.

An athlete who completes the race is recognized as an 'Ironman'. It is intense, exhausting, and exhilarating—trust me, I have done it and loved it! I am an Ironman.

I have a formula that has worked well for me, and I know it can do the same for you. At this time, in this moment, while reading this book, you will discover the knowledge you need to change your life forever. Master these principles, and you will be equipped with the skills you need to make more money, to have more time, and to give yourself real choices. You can take control of your life, and this is the real benefit of becoming financially free.

Over the next few days/weeks, with your permission, I will be your Property Ironman coach while you read this book, and you will learn how to find the ideal location to invest in, the best types of property to buy, and how to buy at a healthy discount.

In addition, you will find out how to add value to your property, how to rent it out to tenants so they pay for your lifestyle, and finally how to recycle your money to buy again and again.

You will learn to overcome many challenges that have been holding you back. It is not a dream; it is completely possible. It does not matter that you work full-time or that you do not have enough money. Great things start from small steps in the right direction.

Do not mistake 'can't' with 'won't.' You have many fears and excuses that need to be addressed if you are going to succeed. Take action and surprise yourself. Step by step, point by point— this book will walk you through the skills you need to develop to become a Property Ironman.

Welcome to the beginning of your success story.

State of the Residential Property Sector

"As the UK housing market downturn gathers pace, it is common for analysts to argue that this downturn will not be as bad as the early 1990s vintage. It looks like it will be worse, perhaps far worse."

ALEX VITILLO, FATHOM CONSULTING

The state of the residential property sector has fluctuated cyclically for decades. Investors, economists, and market commentators always try to predict what is going to happen next in the property market, but they always fail because no one has a crystal ball!

If you are going to learn how to become an Ironman investor, the first step is to orientate yourself in the truth about the property sector. This truth will act as your guiding light, and it will help you make the right purchasing decisions down the line.

The History of Property Investment

The residential property sector has fluctuated for much of the last 40 years. In the mid-1970s the average cost of a new home in the US was $42,500 (source: US Census Bureau New Sales) and in the UK it was £10,728 (source: Nationwide Building Society). In many Western economies in the 1980s house prices rose rapidly as economic performance improved and many people earned enough disposable income to buy their own home or invest in secondary properties

Like it always does, however, the boom was followed by bust. Black Monday in October 1987 saw a collapse in world stock markets and a global recession that hit North America, Europe, Japan, and Australia badly.

Despite growth in some economies, house prices dramatically dropped in many countries and many home owners found themselves in negative equity, where the loan on their house was higher than its value.

The recession lasted until the mid-1990s before house prices, especially in the UK, rose dramatically once again over the next decade. Between 2002 and 2008[1], house prices in the UK rose by 90%, faster than any Eurozone nation, except Spain.

Housing bubbles were reported across many countries in Europe as well as in the USA and Australia, but have fallen again since the 2007 global financial crisis, which we are still trying to recover from today.

So, property within this context is never a sure thing, but you can learn how to stack the odds in your favour if you buy property the right way and follow the system that is outlined in this book.

Property investment has changed. The recent turbulence in the market and general uncertainty about the economy has scared many people away from investing in property.

You cannot rely on the traditional methods to invest in property any more. In this chapter, I am going to show you what you need to do today to get ahead in the property investment game. By doing the opposite of the masses you can significantly increase your wealth. *Pay attention!*

Finance Today, as You Understand It

The world is a pretty tough place, filled with financial catastrophes that never end and that make all our lives pretty difficult. We are in the middle of a deep recession right now that is worse than it was in the 1930s—and the Governor of the Bank of England does not think the repercussions of this global financial crisis will end until after 2016.

There is a European debt crisis arising right now. Pensions pay out nothing, and volatile stock markets make earning

---

1   Lambert, Simon. UK house prices rise at twice Euro average <http://www.thisismoney.co.uk/money/mortgageshome/article-1613567/UK-house-prices-rise-at-twice-Euro-average.html>

an equitable return shaky at best. There is a ton of inflation and lack of financial aid. And each of us is living longer than ever before. The problem?

No one understands how money works or how these problems truly affect them. ALL of these issues in the economy I have just mentioned will impact your life. Finance today, as you understand it, is hopelessly wrong.

Very few can become wealthy by working for someone else. The norm is that you swap your time for money, and time is finite, so most of us work longer and longer hours just to pay the bills. Yet personal debt is at critically high levels because we either use credit cards to pay for the necessities, such as food and fuel, or we use retail therapy to make us feel better and hide from the fact that we are in a recession and life is tough. People want more of everything, and they want it now, on easy payment terms. The money we earn in our J.O.Bs (Just Over Broke) just services the credit card debts that many people have.

We are all forced into this way of living because no-one can afford those little 'luxuries' that we think we deserve, such as a new sofa, new flatscreen TV, or brand new kitchen. They are too expensive. Your full-time job does not allow you to pay for it in cash. Instead, you have to buy it on credit and spend the next five years paying it off.

Money is tight, and in our spend-thrift society we are not taught how to save. Have you ever heard the expression, 'you need money to make money'? This is a twisted version of the correct saying—'money makes money'. In other words, investing in the right things, such as property, should create cash flow for you.

Money is so badly mistreated in our society that people can barely afford to buy food. Together we owe $1.4 trillion in personal debt. Each day in the UK, nearly 300 people are declared insolvent or bankrupt, 1,639 are made redundant and 128 new people per day became unemployed for more than 12 months.

The UK's debt statistics show that on average one person becomes insolvent every four minutes 49 seconds. Michelle Highman of Credit Action says, "*To put this figure into context, it means that in the time it took Mo Farah to win Olympic Gold in the 5,000m, nearly three people went insolvent.*" Every day a whopping 93 properties are repossessed by lenders because of missed payments in the UK. The situation is so bad in the US that entire cities have declared themselves bankrupt.

This never-ending debt cycle means that those who work are making profits for their employers, and while you are working harder and harder for them, you are creating bigger financial problems in your own life. Very few people working 9-5 can afford to become property investors.

You need to clear your personal debt (on store cards, credit cards and personal loans) and stop mismanaging your money by spending now on 'stuff'. Stuff does not buy you financial freedom. Going without now means that you will be able to invest your money wisely—and if you do it right, you will not have to go without ever again. Money should generate more money for you. Put it to work so you do not have to.

Sound good? Read on!

How the Property Sector Has Changed

The property sector is constantly changing and is a barometer to how the whole economy is performing. The good news is that looking at the overall picture proves how important property investment is to your financial health.

There is no doubt that the property market has fluctuated cyclically for decades now, and despite the four recent 'boom and bust' cycles, house prices have grown by an astounding 250% above the general rate of inflation.

This proves that even in turbulent economic times, property remains the number one investment to make on this planet. The demands on property have changed. People aren't simply buying houses to live in anymore.

Like a triathlon that is split into three disciplines, our needs regarding property have been split into three—*necessity, investment, and luxury*.

A simpler way of putting it is to say we buy homes for ourselves, then maybe one or more investment properties, and finally a second or holiday home.

If there is one thing you can depend on when the market cycles so repetitively, it is that those property investors with money are taking advantage of these periods. There are other trends to take note of in the UK housing market.

There has been a growth in home ownership, and an increase in single occupancy households. The quality of home building and craftsmanship has also improved, with the prices of homes increasing annually by 1.8%.

These days, more flats are being built than semi-detached homes and detached homes. According to Nationwide data, a house worth £1,891 in 1952, would be worth around £162,722 today. In 60 years, the average UK house price has actually increased by an average of 7,278%.

When you take a closer look at the overall property market, as I've done for you here, you will see that property has always been a solid investment. Despite the changing markets and economic downturns, property investment done right is still highly lucrative. That is why very wealthy individuals and billion-dollar pension funds invest huge amounts in property.

Demand for housing will always be there, and as our population grows so will house prices. Experts are already forecasting the next boom period, and as the market continues to recover, it will reach a point where buying property is easier for everyone once again.

The Lending Crisis

There is a lending crisis going on in the world right now as banks have restricted how much they lend to people to invest in their businesses and in property. In the UK, and in many other countries, there is a culture of home ownership—it is almost in our psyche.

Over the last 15-20 years when wages rose higher than inflation and the economy was booming, many people started investing in 'buy to let' property.

The property market has always been driven by the availability of financing. With a lending crisis currently in play in the UK, there is very little money being lent making it nearly impossible for many to be able to invest in property.

The Mortgage Crisis

The UK has always had one of the highest home-ownership rates in Europe. But most people cannot afford to pay for their own homes without the help of a mortgage, or they want to use the power of leverage to increase their wealth (more on this later).

It is even more difficult now to get approved for a mortgage, and overall monthly mortgage approvals were 47,312 in the UK in July 2012, less than half the monthly average in the decade to 2007.

As a result, property investors are finding it more difficult to either enter the market or expand their property portfolios.

In many countries today, mortgage lenders have severely restricted who they offer home loans to following the financial crisis. Lenders have tightened their lending criteria by slashing the loan to value (LTV) amount they are prepared to lend against, increasing fees, and increasing borrowing rates.

If you have a great credit rating, a stable income, or a large cash reserve saved up, and are an experienced property landlord, you are more likely to be able to qualify for a mortgage. For those who do not have these benefits, it is very difficult to invest in property.

Sub-Prime Lending

The sub-prime lending crisis was a key reason why the financial crisis hit the US and spread to the rest of the world in 2007.

Typically, you could have got a new mortgage loan quite easily in the early 2000s, even if you didn't fit the standard lending criteria—such as having a provable income! At the same time, many lenders encouraged existing homeowners who were struggling to meet their monthly repayments to remortgage on more favourable terms to boost their business.

Investment banks lumped together thousands of these poorly performing, high risk sub-prime mortgages and sold them in packages called mortgage-backed securities to other institutions and investors around the world.

During the housing and credit boom, demand for these securities grew, which resulted in more lax approvals of mortgage applications being accepted by lenders, which in turn exacerbated the situation further.

When the housing bubble burst, the value of these mortgage-backed securities became almost worthless and trillions of dollars were wiped off the value of US companies. Due to the interconnectedness of global financial institutions, these market losses spread around the world resulting in national governments 'bailing out' many banks, such as Northern Rock in the U.K. and Federal National Mortgage Association (Fannie Mae) in the U.S. Economic growth slowed across the U.S. and Europe, and credit became restricted around the world.

A New Approach to Finance

As lenders have become stricter following the Credit Crunch the only option you have as a Property Ironman is to get creative! Property investors have found new ways of raising the funds they need to build a profitable property portfolio. Although you have to jump through more hoops to get a mortgage approved from a bank these days, they are still lending and they are a great source of finance.

Most buy to let mortgages will lend at 75% loan to value, meaning that you can get a £75,000 mortgage on a property worth £100,000, in other words you only have to find £25,000 to buy an asset worth four times as much.

What's more is that the banks do their own checks and balances in the form of an independent valuation to ensure that the property you want to buy is a good investment— this gives you further peace of mind if you know what to buy and how to turn your property into a cash machine.

Of course, you will need enough funds to pay for the deposit and fees, but if you do not have enough cash this is where the new approach to finance can help.

Believe it or not, there are plenty of alternative ways of getting enough cash to become a Property Ironman, if you just know where to look. If you have lived in your current home for a while, the chances are that you might have a significant amount of equity in your property that you could release through a remortgage to start buying investment property.

If that is you, check that the increased costs of borrowing money from your own home is affordable, and the income that your investments can realistically generate is more than the increased costs. If they are, then you have found a lump of cash that can pay for the buy to let mortgage deposit, fees, and refurbishment (if that is your chosen strategy— more on that later).

Friends, family, and other investors are another great source of joint venture finance to start building your property portfolio. Using other people's money is a great way to get started in property or even to accelerate the growth of your existing property portfolio. To attract investor's money, you need to be credible.

In other words, you need to know what you are doing. So it is best to get yourself educated first (I'm certain this book will help you!)

Once you have found a strategy that appeals, spend time researching how you can make it work in your local area. If you become the local 'expert' and can demonstrate that you know what you're doing, you will find it easier to ask friends and family for funding. You might offer your time and expertise to buy a deal and refurbish it to add value in return for your friend's money. Once you have one deal behind you, it'll give you loads of confidence to speak to more people and ask for their money too!

If you are increasingly frustrated that your life is in a rut, you work long hours so you never see your loved ones, you get passed over for promotions, or you never have any spare money at the end of the month, then investing like a Property Ironman is the key to increasing your long-term wealth.

Taking Control of Your Finances

There are two things you need to know about taking control of your finances. First of all, it is an on-going process. There is no point where you will be able to say, 'okay my finances are completely 100%.' Secondly, money can come and go very quickly if you take your finger off the pulse for just a moment.

We live in a consumerist world. We are taught that we can have whatever we want now, as long as we pay for it every month. So, we impulse buy. Then we spend the next three years regretting that decision. It is a cycle of debt that has many people trapped.

While you might not be able to get a mortgage with your credit score, you can bet that you can get any clothing, furniture, or retail account on offer. The debt quickly adds up and can take over your entire salary.

We buy because we are frustrated with our lives, just cannot stop ourselves, everyone has that 'thing' and you don't want to be left behind, or because we hate our jobs. Then we are locked into jobs we hate because we owe others for the things we've bought. It is very destructive isn't it?

In today's ridiculous world, either you man (or woman) up and take responsibility for your finances or the system will trap you. The unfortunate joke is that millions of people do not even realize that they are being trapped!

They live in a delirious state waiting for the SYSTEM to correct itself and improve their lives.

'If I get that promotion, things will get better.'

'If I improve my credit score, then I can afford that car I want.' 'If I can secure a loan from the bank, I can finally move into my own home.'

Each one of these thoughts is reliant on an untrustworthy system. YOU are the person who comes off second best when the system once again does something bad or just carries on as normal. Another mortgage crisis, another recession....you need to prepare yourself and your family for these.

If anything, taking control of your finances is the one thing we MUST all do to achieve success in this crazy economic climate. It's also the one thing that 99.99% of people never do. I am here to help you set yourself free and to show you another way.

This book is about getting your own back. It is about addressing your finances, improving them, and then becoming financially free. The Property Ironman philosophy is a way of life. You will need it if you are going to go against the system and do what most people are not able or willing to do, and that's to secure your own wealth.

You can be a leader who shines as a beacon to others. They will see what you have achieved, and some might want to follow suit. Others will resent you for it or might think you 'just got lucky'. It will be a hard and treacherous road, but you'll be rewarded beyond anything you would have received if you had not taken that first step to becoming a Property Ironman.

Every pound you earn should come from something that you have done for yourself. Enough passing the buck (pound or euro), and enough excuses. You do not have to be the spectator sitting on the side lines anymore wondering how the Ironmen were able to overcome the odds and win the race. The race has always been yours.

You have the starting gun. You choose your opponents and your team. You decide how much you win, WHEN you win.

The Consequences of Ignoring Property Investing

In life, you are always surrounded by consequences. Those shoes that you bought last week looked great, but now they hurt your feet. That chocolate bar that you stowed away in your shopping trolley has now been eaten, and if you are anything like me, you feel guilty!

Whether the decisions are little or large, we make them every day, and in so doing, set ourselves up for either success or failure. Buying chocolate to keep in your home while you're on a diet almost guarantees that you will break your diet. It's a decision you made, but you know this stuff already.

There are consequences of ignoring property investment. I think we can all agree that the common denominator in any wealthy person's portfolio is the sheer amount of property that he or she owns. Property is the fastest, most direct route to wealth and financial freedom.

Becoming wealthy in other ways is SO rare that less than one percent of people in the UK are able to do it. Even they buy property. It is a way to ensure that your money is safe. It is a way to guarantee that you will have passive income forever. More than 40% of *The Times* annual '100 Rich List' have built their fortunes through property investment, so why doesn't everyone follow their example?

The consequences of doing nothing are not pretty. Financial insecurity is everywhere. You have already experienced it with your parents or older friends—haven't you?

Their pensions do not cover their cost of living. They are either still working or have had to sell everything they own to make ends meet. They, along with millions of other Baby Boomers, have lost everything to the system that they thought would provide for them in their old age.

The system told them—'work hard, spend, save a bit, be a loyal employee, pay your pension.' They did what they were told, and in many cases it amounted to nothing. Imagine what the system is telling all of us to do now that will negatively affect us when we reach retirement age?

Did you know that if you have built up a £100,000 pension pot over your working life it would only pay you about £4,000 PER YEAR? If you had to rely on that income in your retirement, that would put you way under the poverty line. I do not know about you, but many people need £4,000 *per month* just to pay for their mortgage, food, car, utility bills, clothing, and entertainment.

The consequences of financial insecurity are bleak and harsh. You will never get to travel. You will never own something completely. You will never stop worrying about money. You will not be able to give your children or your parents a better life. You will always have to live life on the cheap.

Everything is affected by wealth—including your health and happiness. Property investing is the only way you are going to rise above this gloomy future. If you do manage to master it, and earn your own financial freedom, your life will change.

I cannot begin to explain to you what it feels like to spend time with my family, guilt-free. I am there at all the important moments in my children's lives. To NOT have to worry about money. To be able to take my family and friends on holidays when we need it. To work because I WANT to work not because I NEED to work is a very liberating feeling.

It is something you should reach for with every fibre of your being. Once you have it, the opportunities in your life quadruple. There is nothing you cannot achieve. Suddenly you have a freedom that most people never get to experience in their lives. It's well worth fighting to get.

That is why you need to become a Property Ironman.

My Personal Story: Race to the Top

Fulfilment is one of those things that people forget about because life is so hard. We forget that without fulfilment, marriages fall apart, careers become dismantled, friends fall away, and our lives become total disasters.

We spend most of our lives working—that's the reality. I got to a point in my life where my job just didn't do it for me anymore. Over ten years I helped create the most successful division in our global business but at the expense of working long hours, hardly ever seeing my family, and missing countless important events in my children's lives. I built up a powerful sales team only to be asked to make almost everyone one of them redundant when the Credit Crunch struck. That was stressful and depressing. One of the methods I began to use to deal with my daily stresses was exercise.

Shortly after my 37th birthday, I met a friend who convinced me to join a local triathlon club just to try something different. I could not swim a length of a 25 metre pool without stopping, and when out cycling I was the one who got left behind even on the smallest hill climb, but I began to enjoy it nonetheless. It was also an escape from my corporate prison. Within the first season I completed my first 'Sprint' triathlon in 1 hour and 10 minutes —no records were broken that day, but it was a great feeling to compete and to finish.

I completed over a dozen triathlons in the following two years before a buddy of mine, an Irishman called Bernie Murphy, talked me into doing an Ironman triathlon one Christmas over a pint down the pub. Complete naivety (and a few drinks) meant I'd agreed to do it before I even knew what an Ironman triathlon was!

We had just over eight months until August 2011 to train for this mammoth event and neither of us had a clue where to start. The sheer thought of it filled me with dread, especially as the event we had entered was in the French Alps and had more than 5,000m of mountain climbs! I live in one of the flattest counties in England, and the steepest climb is probably the gentle slope of my driveway where it meets the road outside my house.

Early on Bernie passed me a great book called *Be Iron Fit* by Don Fink that outlined a systematic approach to training over a 30-week period. Don had completed many Ironman races including the ultimate event, the Hawaii Ironman at Kona, and certainly knows his stuff. We gradually built up the time spent training on swimming, cycling, and running, using the recommended schedule every week. The time spent training became manageable, and it even became enjoyable (after about four months!)

We managed to fit in the training into our busy lives, and I felt happier and more able to cope with the pressures of corporate life as the months went by. At 6am on the August 14, more than 1,000 wetsuit-clad athletes waited in the darkness by the shores of the lake for the signal to start Embrunman 2011. Almost 17 hours later after bouts of exhaustion, a bike crash, and delirium I crossed the finish line with Bernie in 790ᵗʰ place, and I was the happiest man alive!

It was without a doubt the most physically challenging and exhausting thing I have ever done. It was also the most rewarding.

By finishing that race, I proved to myself that I could do things beyond the norm, that I had the power to make things happen in my own life. There was a moment when I felt relieved. I let myself off the hook. It was not my fault that my life had not gone to plan. First of all, I did not have a plan—I was blindly following a plan that society told me to follow.

Despite the heat, pain, mountains, and exhaustion I knew what was coming. I knew where I was going. I knew to get there I needed to pedal for another few hours, then run for five hours. The route was mapped out for me. I would only fail if I allowed myself to give up. I had confidence in myself because I had diligently followed a proven training system that I knew would get me by. What's more is that I did not want to let Bernie down.

And friends, that's exactly what being a professional property investor is all about. It can be a gruelling process, with ups and downs, highs and lows. You can even hit a wall, but the key is to push past and keep on going because you will succeed.

Life is a race to the top. Competing in Ironman events taught me that. If I did not invest in my body, I would never finish the race. In life, we are discouraged from investing in ourselves. But that is the first thing you need to do to make sense of everything.

I began investing in property seven years ago. At the time I did not know much about managing money or property. But I knew the principles, and I learned everything else over time. For a triathlete, the challenges are to become efficient in the three core disciplines—swimming, cycling, and running.

Becoming great at property investment requires the same process—becoming efficient in the three core disciplines: *finance, property*, and *investment*.

Without doubt the most profitable properties I've bought have been in the last 18 months. In these terrible economic times, when lending has been a challenge, I have continued to buy discounted properties that rent out and generate a significant monthly profitable income for my family.

A short while ago I reviewed my finances and realized that I had made enough sound property investments to make myself and my family financially secure, forever. I don't say this to impress anyone; in fact, I'm extremely grateful for what I've learnt and achieved, and to those that have helped me get there, but I want to prove to everyone that they can do this for themselves too.

I'm still competing in Ironman races, and I will always invest in property to increase my wealth—but I do not need to work at all. My wife does not have to work. We choose to work, and what we choose to do is always a passion of ours. *That's life fulfilment.*

The Property Ironman has been written so you too can learn from my proven system and implement the steps required to achieve financial freedom for your loved ones.

Winning the Gold: Key Beliefs and Framework

"I wasn't satisfied just to earn a good living. I was looking to make a statement."

DONALD TRUMP

Getting out of the rat race system that forces us to rely on lenders and banks is what I like to call 'winning the gold.' To do this, you need to develop an entirely new perspective from the one you've been operating with your entire life.

Let's agree that the old system that you are caught up in right now is not working for you! Instead, it is time to develop key beliefs that will help you overcome this limited way of thinking and behaving so that you can excel and become a Property Ironman.

These frameworks will be the stepping stones that you will use to become a dominant force in the property investment arena. I will go into detail on each of these key beliefs as I outline them for you here.

The Financial Triathlete: Six Key Beliefs

Becoming a financial triathlete means that your new ambition in life is to adopt and develop these six key beliefs. You cannot hope to succeed without them, and I will tell you why.

#1: The Medallist Mindset

Having the right mindset is not only essential to becoming a Property Ironman, it is also the first and most basic requirement. Your mind controls what you believe, what you think, how you act, and what you do when things do not go as planned. You will need expert control of it if you are going to become a pro property investor.

#2: Goals for a Sprint Finish

The ability to set goals carefully and efficiently is one of the best skills you will ever learn to hone in your life. When you apply this in property investment, you will learn to move smoothly from objective to objective, slowly building yourself a property empire that continually builds up your overall wealth.

#3: Focus on the Course

Developing the ability to focus on the most important elements of your strategies is a supportive skill that you can rely on. People who are able to focus on something properly are able to reach their goals sooner and complete them efficiently. In property investment, focus can save you a lot of money in the long run.

#4: The Persistent Swimmer

Persistence is a trait that everyone has, but few develop. It is really a super power in property investing, and it is the key mechanism in gaining industry and practical knowledge. Being persistent is perhaps the most important key belief that you will learn. The good news is that it can be developed to the point where you never fail at anything again.

#5: Team Gold

Building a reliable team of people to help you achieve this success is an essential ingredient in becoming a Property Ironman. There isn't a wealthy person in the world who achieved all of their wealth alone. It is an ingredient many leave out, which is why you still find self-employed and hardworking people struggling to make ends meet.

#6: The Ambitious Cyclist

Ambition is the final key belief, and it will keep you reaching for bigger and better opportunities. Never underestimate the power of ravenous ambition!

The Medallist Mindset

Have you ever heard that old adage, 'your attitude determines your altitude?' It's clever, and what's more—it's 100% right. Your attitude is directly linked to your mindset.

To become a powerhouse Property Ironman, you need to adopt the medallist mindset.

A medallist triathlete is someone who has been training for years and has completed dozens of Ironman events. When they compete, they are able to outperform everyone in the race and exceed their own personal best.

For this to happen, they need to adopt the mindset of a winner. There is only so much you can do as an athlete to get yourself physically fit. That is why experts say that it is not necessarily the fastest runner who wins, but the one who WANTS it the most.

Right now, you are the athlete in the triathlon who swims the entire distance of the first leg, and then gives up when you reach the opposite shore because you're tired. Believe it or not, being 'tired' is pretty much the reason people give up on things.

An athlete with a positive, pro-active mindset who is out to WIN the race isn't ever going to entertain the idea of quitting. In property investment, this mindset will help you win and set you up for the rest of your life. You might not be competing with a few hundred other investors for the same property, but you'll find that there is always opposition in some form standing in your way.

Most often, it is your own mental attitude. The 'I can't afford it' attitude or the 'it's going to fail' attitude or the 'I'm not good enough' attitude. We are taught from a young age to fear failure, when the term has no real meaning in property investment.

Failure only happens when you allow it to happen because mentally you've decided that this is the course you want to take. Notice how I say 'want to' and not 'have to.' A property investor who is motivated never makes excuses.

The medallist mindset you need to adopt will teach you how to get out of that water, exhausted, get on a bike, and feverishly pedal for HOURS, only to run like crazy towards the finish line. Only when you have hit that tape and won the gold will you slow down and stop.

Let me tell you about Paul, a friend of mine who I met last year. He has a young family, works hard for a local I.T. company, and desperately wanted to invest in property because he's watched numerous shows on TV that make it look easy to earn a fortune through property. He really liked the property auction programmes and thought that was for him so he went along to his local auction house. After getting caught up in all the excitement of the bidding he 'won' Lot number 29, which was a three bed bungalow on the other side of town in need of some attention.

Paul was ecstatic at getting his first investment property but also nervous about what to do next. Unfortunately, Paul had not done a survey on the property before the auction and ended up buying a building that looked great on the outside and had potential, but also had so many structural problems that he could not afford to carry out the additional works to rectify. Despite an offer by his brother to loan him the money, Paul did not want to feel beholden to him in case he could not make a profit so felt he had no choice but to put the bungalow back into the next auction. He sold it to an experienced investor for a knock-down price and Paul lost almost £19,000 (or $31,000) on the sale.

Despite his early enthusiasm, I doubt Paul will ever invest in property again because he didn't feel equipped to overcome the problems that faced him and he lost most of his hard-earned savings. The fact is that he could have made money on this investment if he had prepared properly and knew who to ask and what to do.

This lesson should teach you something about property investment. It is a real science, and it requires a positive outlook at all times. Sometimes you might make some bad investments, but if you do your due diligence the right way, you will stack the cards in your favour and become a successful Property Ironman.

You will compete in many property sales. One by one, you will add extra cash to your income streams. Only when you have reached the finish line—the tape of financial freedom—can you slow down. Until then, you are a blink of an eye away from falling back into the 'easy' life of having a J.O.B. The sad thing is that so many people give up when they are so close to the finish line – they just don't realise it.

I know that my attitude contributed to my success in property and as a triathlete and it pulled me through all the trials, errors, and doubts. Without a medallist mindset, I never would have won the proverbial gold.

Goals for a Sprint Finish

The second key belief that I want to expand on is goal setting. I call it 'goals for a sprint finish' and here's why.

I was given a really great piece of advice by a friend of mine who had been doing triathlons for a lot longer than I had. We were speaking about the next event and improving on our personal best times.

Now, there is nothing quite like the end stretch of track or road or dirt when you are about to finish the triathlon.

You are exhausted beyond belief, and so in the zone that a herd of stampeding cattle would not be able to knock you off your path. That friend gave me an amazing piece of advice that allowed me to improve my time in that home stretch. The last event that I did was a half-marathon; I felt really strong in the final few miles of the run and sprinted for the finish line with 800m to go. Although I thought I was going to puke, I got a personal best and knocked four minutes off my best run time!

Do you know what he told me?

He said I needed to set mental goals for myself. Close to the end of every training session, I'd mentally prepare myself for a final sprint. For three minutes I would go all out—as fast as I could— until reaching the mental marker (hopefully without puking!) before resuming a steady pace again.

It became clear that setting these mini goals in my training became especially beneficial in the home stretch of that last race. I would place a LOT better because for the final five minutes of the final run—I could sprint to the finish. This takes a lot of discipline and mental preparation, but it works.

You can liken this to property investment. It is tempting to have a slow and steady approach to everything. But sometimes you just have to take action and go for it. Goals help you do that.

When you become a master goal-setter, you will be able to break down key tasks or rearrange your perspective in ways you never thought possible.

Goals are also great for prioritizing your life. In property investment, goals can lead you to bigger rewards. Effective goals always come with time limits, and these can be the most helpful of all because they put you under pressure to achieve them by a specific date. Do not forget that a well thought out goal coupled with a great blueprint-like plan is all you need for imminent success.

My first property goal was to buy four properties in the first year and increase my net monthly income by at least £1,000. I just about had enough money to pay for two house deposits, the legal fees and a small refurb, but that was it. Over those 12 months I kept my goal in mind and came up with creative ways to get the money needed to buy three more property deals. I achieved my initial goal, and it's amazing the confidence boost this gave me.

You can do this too. Make sure that your goals are relevant and that they serve the bigger picture. Try to keep them in the confines of reality, but do not be afraid to dream big! Check your goals against each other—sometimes they can be contradictory.

To get your sprint finish in property investment means that you'll have to first set many smaller goals that will accelerate your pace. Stick to them, and soon you'll find that you've reached that home stretch. One or two more choice investments, and you will be in your sprint finish. Make it count!

Focus on the Course

Focus is perhaps the most difficult of all of these key beliefs. Just doing something does not mean that you are focused on it. We live in a society where distraction is exalted and focus is discouraged. We not only want information, pictures, video, entertainment or gratification instantly but are bombarded with hundreds and thousands of bits of information every day, whether that's via email, post, TV, text, radio, or talking to others. It's very difficult to shut off this constant stream of distraction. I personally have found learning to focus one of the hardest skills to perfect. But you can do it; everyone can with a bit of effort, and you will be amazed at how much more productive and successful you will become.

There are many different levels of focus. For me in Ironman, I find I perform to my best when I focus on my technique during races. For me, being focused on what I can control and drowning out any other thoughts or distractions that might have been detrimental to what I was doing has worked.

When I swim, I focus on each stroke and every breath. When I cycle, the elliptical motion and the pressure in my feet and legs are all that mattered. When I run, staying relaxed in the hands, shoulders and face is all that I care about. But a small part of me is also focused on the task at hand—staying apart from the other competitors and being aware of the course.

When there is a bicycle pile-up, as can happen around tight bends in the course for example, if you are lucky you can normally avoid it by focusing on the track rather than the other competitors. If you watch the Tour de France bike race, you will see how often these professional cyclists have huge crashes, sometimes wiping out up to half the peleton. Fractionally losing focus can result in your race being over. The same can be said for property investment. If you are focused on making that great investment, you will not allow yourself to fall for sales pitches, and you will be able to see past nice furnishings and glossy brochures. Remember that ugly houses often make great investments—but more on that later!

A big part of maintaining your focus is having well defined goals. Goals keep you on track. You should define your strategy and set goals yourself before you race out to find properties to buy. Being focused on your goals also means tracking your overall progress to see that you're doing what needs to be done to succeed. I cannot tell you how many times I almost got ahead of myself, thinking about investing in a new area or one a different type of property only to pull back because I was veering off my chosen strategic path.

There are so many shiny new property investing strategies sold by people who say they are making millions from them that this can be incredibly distracting and can cause you to procrastinate at best and divert your efforts at worst. My advice to anyone is find one strategy, focus on implementing what you need to do to become successful at it, and keep repeating it. If it ain't broke....

Being focused in property investment also means making certain things more important than others and planning ahead for them. In life, as in property investment, the course we take is really a direct result of where our focus lies. I find that understanding the thing that drives me (my reason WHY) helps me keep focus too. For me, providing for my family is my WHY, and I have a picture of them above my desk to make sure I do not lose focus on what's important.

An athlete who competes in an Ironman event while full of distraction, uncertainty, or frustration may never finish the race. They have to clear their minds, so that the only thing they are focused on is swimming, cycling, running, finishing. It is so easy to become distracted by things in life that will negatively affect your focus.

And when you are not focused on a goal, things slip by you. I learned this the hard way before I had educated myself in property when I bought an amazing off-plan apartment in 2005. When it was finished, it was a great apartment but it ended up taking months to rent out because there were so many other new properties that had been released onto the market at the same time. I was so engrossed by its potential that I hastily snapped it up, before doing any research on the ability to achieve the rent quoted by the sales company. Because of my lack of focus, I had just spent over the odds on an apartment that was not going to make me any money for at least a dozen years!

Keep your focus, bear in mind your reason why, and do not make emotional investment decisions.

The Persistent Swimmer

Persistence, as I mentioned earlier in the chapter, is perhaps the most important of all the key beliefs that lead to property investment success. There are thousands of stories out there about business people and athletes who only 'got it right' on their ninth or tenth try. Thomas Edison, the inventor of the electric light bulb, is quoted as saying 'I have not failed. I've just found 10,000 ways that don't work!'

It's so easy to get caught up in the failure mindset. We think that if we do not do something perfectly the first time, we have failed and we are out of chances. Well, being persistent is incredibly important in Ironman races.

If you have ever swum a very long distance, you will know what I'm talking about. There comes a point when you've gone too far to turn back, but you feel too tired to keep going. It's the first real wall you have to get over in order to make it back to dry land.

In this case, you only really have one option—to keep swimming. And there is a real lesson in there for me about property investment. A persistent property investor will get much further in this career than one who treads carefully, is full of doubt, and does not keep going. These are the people who 'dabble' for a while before quitting.

You cannot set a goal to be more persistent. You have no choice in that water; it is either keep swimming or sink—that is how you should react to things in life that test you. Make a decision to never stop trying, and persistence will become your greatest ally.

You will find in your property investing career that you are tested regularly in this regard. There will be plenty of opportunities for you to quit in the early days. If you are conscious that these moments are learning curves, you can choose to be persistent, adapt your approach and move forward, you will achieve your property goals.

Persistence comes from inside—it is that internal voice that re-fuels and reenergizes your body. When you are running on that first kilometre, and you've just completed a 180 kilometre cycle ride, persistence is all you have left. In Ironman events athletes are rewarded with great placements, medals, new personal bests and that satisfying feeling of a job well done.

Nothing is hard if focus and persistence are working in your favour. You will find that taking the first steps to becoming a Property Ironman is easy once your mind is made up about it. Do not let yourself get away with being average. Be extraordinary!

Team Gold

It takes a team to make an athlete great. It also takes a team to make a successful Property Ironman. Too often, we are taught to strike out on our own and become rich. But no one in the world has ever become rich on their own. It ALWAYS takes team work.

The faster you get your team together, the better off you will be—and this is why. In Ironman events, initially you just want to finish proving to yourself that you can step up to the challenge. Then you might want to become better, to achieve a new personal best or even win the race.

So, you hire a coach for each sport to help with your technique, a personal trainer to improve your overall conditioning, a dietician to make sure you are eating the best things needed to fuel your body, and a physiotherapist to keep you in one piece! You might start training with a few friends to make it more enjoyable and to keep the competitive juices flowing.

At the end of it all—you have employed the help of a dozen people to whip you into shape for the next Ironman event.

This is your Power Team or you Team Gold. They help prepare you for the act of competing in the race. This is exactly what your support team should be doing in your property investment business. Many first-time property investors find a place they like, look at it, and then they buy it. Inexperienced buyers often make costly mistakes and don't know who to turn to for advice.

A savvy newbie Property Ironman will create their Team Gold first before they start buying. Their team might include a number of estate agents, a legal team, a refurbishment team, an architect, a letting agent and an independent surveyor. Leveraging the time and expertise of your Team Gold is just great business and will accelerate your success.

It is a symbiotic relationship that is mutually beneficial. Team Gold will shape you into a lean, mean, property accumulating machine!

Start by letting go of the idea that you are an island. You can become successful on your own, but it is a lot harder and it can be lonely to chart your own course. Team Gold will accelerate your pace and improve your chances of success. They are the ones standing by the side of the road handing out fresh cups of water and words of encouragement to keep you going. Without them, your chances of giving up increase exponentially.

It is important to hand-pick your team, so take your time and explain what you want and need from them. You might not get it right straight away, but by building your Team Gold you will help ensure you achieve financial freedom and become a Property Ironman in double-quick time.

The Ambitious Cyclist

Up until now, you have been drifting through life, going from one job to the next, never really doing anything you love, never really going anywhere in your career. You need to become like the ambitious cyclist. There is nothing more terrifying that finding yourself in a group of high speed cyclists and feeling out of your depth.

You have people in front of you and people behind you. There are cyclists on either side of you. You are completely blocked in. If you stopped, or slowed down, or hesitated, or turned in the wrong direction—all of those people would tumble from their seats in a massive heap of carbon, wheels and Lycra.

All of these people are ambitious cyclists. They are willing to take the risk of crashing because huddling together in each other's slip streams accelerates their speed and reduces the effort they expend. To become an ambitious cyclist, you need to reclaim your right to be ambitious. Reach for what you want, and don't be afraid of wanting it.

People who give into their fear hesitate and crash. People who are too afraid to join the throng of high speed bikes get left behind. Be the ambitious cyclist in the very front, taking the most risk of all once you have prepared yourself adequately for the task ahead. Ambition is exactly what you need to be a highly effective property investor.

Property Ironmen attack what they want with keen ambition, and like that leading cyclist, will not stop until they have secured first place in the race. If you see a property you want, do your research and go for it.

Funnily enough, ambition requires patience. It is easy to become over-ambitious and to rush ahead with things without thinking. Buying up un-researched property deals on a whim is a fool's game.

What tends to happen is that all of these key beliefs come together to make you into the perfect Property Ironman. You taste success, and you cannot wait to get more of it. Then something happens. Over ambition! You become reckless (or lazy) with your money, your team, and your properties. Do not fall into that trap!

So, ambition and focus are vital attributes for the successful property investor. The trick to staying ambitious is maintaining motivation. Motivation can wane, so remember to refuel it with reward and persistence, always keeping in mind your reason 'Why'.

If you add all of these amazing Property Ironman beliefs together, you have the ingredients you need for success. People who develop these beliefs are the ones who become successful.

The Winning 3PR Framework

I have told you what you need to work on as a person. Now here is the proven framework that you need to make all of those traits come together. I call it the 'winning 3PR framework,' and it looks like this.

The 3 Ps

First up are the three Ps of property investment. This financial success formula has been tried and tested by me personally, and it works.

1. **Place: Where to Buy** – When you know where to buy, your path to financial freedom will become a

lot easier. Investment is all about choosing the right location. From where it is to which direction it faces—all the factors must be added up here. Knowing where to buy will save you time, effort, and money.

2. **Property: What to Buy** – When you know what to buy, it drastically improves your chances of creating long-term wealth. In the beginning, property will seem like a confusing choice between commercial or residential property, terraced houses, detached properties, or flats. Getting 'Property' right will set you up for life.

3. **Pro Team: Your Power Pro Team** – When you know who to trust and rely on, property investment becomes a piece of cake. Build yourself a reliable team of people who you can leverage their time and expertise to help you succeed. Building networks of contacts and finding a mentor is also a crucial step in the process.

The 3 Rs

After the three Ps, come the three Rs—they are equally as important, and they teach you what to do with the property once you've attained it.

1. **Refurbish: Touch Ups and Tricks** – Buying at the best price and then increasing the value of property through refurbishing it determines how much money you make. Doing this wisely and shrewdly will maximise your profit.

2. **Rent: Financing Your Lifestyle** – Finding the right tenants to live in your property can be a challenge. I will show you how to do it right so that they not only look after your property but pay for your lifestyle too.

3. Refinance: Recycle Your Cash – Learn how to refinance your properties so that you can release most or all of the cash you invested in them in order to buy more and create more wealth. This is the sensible and sustainable way that Property Ironmen build long-term financial freedom.

Using the Winning 3PR framework will help you quickly and easily find, fix, and refinance properties to build a solid asset that not only grows in value but also pays you an income each and every month.

This is a simple model, and it is easy for anyone to replicate. The more you work the 3PR framework, the more it will work for you!

Step 1: Place – Where To Buy

"Wide diversification is only required when investors do not understand what they are doing."

WARREN BUFFET

Figuring out where to invest in property is the first step in the Property Ironman process. Place has so much impact on your financial goals and on the property that you purchase that it is the foundation of the 3PR buying framework.

Finding the right location to invest in will save you time, effort, and money. Picking the wrong place to buy can be very costly, so please read on to ensure you do not make the same mistake as so many other newbie investors.

Your Location Selection

Have you heard the phrase 'location, location, location'? What does it mean to you? Some people think it is about investing in property in the centre of a city; others think it is about buying the worst house in the best street; but to me it is more basic than that.

Have you seen the property sections in the weekend newspapers? They are full of glossy features and pictures about luxury properties in exotic locations, whether that's a ski chalet in the Swiss Alps, an exclusive beach hut in the Caribbean or a weekend retreat in a beautiful European city. The features all look incredible, and they report on endless examples of people who are living their dream lifestyle having given up their stressful lives back home.

Do not fall for it! The property pages and television programmes about buying abroad are designed to help you forget about your daily reality...and to help you part with your hard-earned savings. Please forgive my cynicism, but I have seen many people lose money this way and I do not want you to fall into the same trap.

Mark Homer is a friend of mine who bought a ski chalet in Bulgaria a number of years ago. It was an 'off-plan' development that was not even built yet (see Chapter 4: Property - What To Buy) and the salesman showed him lots of glossy brochures about how the ski resort would look when finished, as well as rental projections from the hordes of ski tourists who would be making their annual pilgrimage to the slopes.

Mark thought he had done his due diligence; Bulgaria was an up and coming destination having joined the Eurozone after all - and paid his deposit and fees. A year later he was told the resort was finished, but over the next 12 months the only person who rented his chalet was his best friend who went for a week, and even that was at a discounted 'mates rates' price! When Mark finally had enough and visited the resort, he clearly saw that it bore little resemblance to the glossy brochures. Nothing was finished, dozens of chalets and the hotel were empty, and he realised his mistake. He had paid an inflated price for a property that was thousands of miles away from home and was reliant on local 'experts' to manage it for him. Mark later sold that Bulgarian ski chalet at a €50,000 LOSS and vowed never to buy abroad again.

Now do not get me wrong, buying your dream holiday home abroad can be a wonderful thing and it might even make you some money, but it is not going to provide you a passive income stream for the rest of your life. This is one of the reasons why I have written *The Property Ironman:* to try to stop you making the same mistake that Mark and thousands of others like him make every year. When you have become a successful property investor, you do not have to work anymore, and have the passive income that you want, then go ahead and invest abroad, but please do not do it before then!

Old vs. New Location Research

It was only a few years ago that many parts of the world were enjoying unprecedented economic growth. As mentioned in the Introduction, incomes were relatively high and millions had enough disposable income to take a few international holidays each year. As the global economic outlook was generally positive, demand for property increased dramatically, especially from the growing middle classes. Mortgage lending was abundant and buying abroad was a relatively cheap and easy process. It did not matter what price you paid for your investment because as property prices continued to inflate those who had bought abroad were sitting on handsome 'paper profits.' The global economic downturn and Credit Crunch burst the property bubbles in almost every country and wiped out those paper profits, leaving many international investors with rising costs, negative equity, and no renters for their properties.

I know this is a simplistic description about what happened, but the results are the same however you want to complicate it. Millions of people are in an even worse financial situation than before because they invested without thinking about cash-flow and bought property at the wrong price and in the wrong location.

It is imperative in today's world to invest with your eyes open and pick your location with cash-flow in mind. Forget the glossy brochures and television programmes in the sun, buy locally, and invest in where you know to build up your passive income.

You absolutely have to become a solid area researcher if you are going to become a Property Ironman. It is like preparing for the bike stretch in your triathlon. If you don't research the best ways to overcome the terrain and to stick hard to the many bends and twists in the road—you are never going to beat your personal best time.

Research helps you prepare for success in the future. That's why it is an important part of your property investment strategy. Wise investors will tell you that the more you know about an area, the better your property choices will be.

If I want to buy a property in a local town, you need to uncover everything you can about the place first. Who typically lives in this neighbourhood? Are there lots of families with children, young adults, or older people in the neighbourhood? What sort of homes do my potential tenants want and what can they afford? What is the crime rate like?

When you learn where the best areas are, you tend to pick out winning locations that are situated on highly lucrative streets. The three bedroom terrace homes I rent to people are nearly always in family-orientated areas; lots of parks, schools, and amenities.

Much of your property's worth will be determined by location, so learn to be picky and questioning now—it may save you some financial losses down the road. Invest in a great location, and you'll very likely enjoy some high returns.

A great location does not necessarily mean that it is the sort of area that you would want to live in yourself because often the best value properties are found in 'cheaper' areas. If an area looks a bit rundown but is improving, demand to live there is high and prices are relatively low, investigate it further. Buying at a substantial discount below market value will lock in your profits and give you a great asset over the long-term. But how do you find these areas?

Research is so much easier today compared to 15 or 20 years ago because of the modern digital world that we live in where information is literally at our fingertips. You can do the bulk of your research online and it is easy to compare and contract multiple locations before picking your chosen location. This only takes a few hours, and it can help eliminate so many novice mistakes, ensuring that you will create the passive income that you want.

Back in 1990, there was no Internet that could assist in the property location search. Instead, you would have to get your information from direct sources or by speaking to people on the telephone.

If you wanted to find out if an area was a good investment, you would visit that area and spend time there finding out all you could. Now, while this is an older method of research, it's also still one of the more accurate ways to gauge whether a potential location is worth your time or not.

I would recommend using this method when you are about to finalize your decision about a specific location because you want to 'sanity check' your findings and get a real feel for the place, but you should still do all the main information gathering online or over the phone. Remember, we are trying to save you time and effort in picking the right location, so leverage the electronic resources around you.

Location research means including collected data that is shared online to help you form your investment opinion. Towns and cities also have their own websites now, and the local council housing pages can provide a wealth of information on local housing strategy documents, housing demand, and rental prices.

In addition, governmental statistical websites will tell you population size, socio-demographic data, employment data and relative size of the local economy for the location you are researching. These statistics may include growth patterns over a period of several years, crime rates, community details, and nuggets of information about the area infrastructure.

All of these pieces of the puzzle come together to form your complete picture of the area.

Specialist property portals might have compiled much of this information already, so they are worth looking out for. Examples in the UK include Zoopla and Land Registry, but you can use Google or Yahoo to find local sites.

There are even property databases online that you can access, which will provide you with additional information about the area. It is easy to get caught up in the modern age's facts and figures—and to forget about the simple act of asking someone's opinion about something. But when you combine these two methods, good things happen.

A simple way for a Property Ironman to get an insider's view on any area you are researching is to ask local property experts. If you know any local successful property investors, ask them for advice. Tell them you are just researching the area and want to find out from the best how they have done it. You might be surprised at how generous people are at sharing their knowledge, especially if it involves talking about themselves! If you do not know any investors, find a local property networking event and ask people there. These events only cost about £10 to attend and are held around the country every month—you can do an online search to find the closest one to you.

Another approach is to talk to three or four local estate agents and letting agents. They can be a mine of useful information if you ask the right questions, and in this economic environment are often desperate to sell houses so they are keen to help you as much as possible.

Asking a selection of agents should give you a balanced view of your potential investment area.

If you come across as a potential client, they hope you might make them sales commission. Ask them what are the best areas to invest in and why they think that. Also, ask them where NOT to invest and why. Knowing where not to invest in your chosen area is just as valuable to you. It not only helps broaden your knowledge about the area, but it can help save money because you are more likely to invest only in those streets that best fit your strategy.

When you compare these local opinions a lot of good information can come to light. If that fails, hit the streets! What I mean is—go from shop to shop, or from door to door—and ask the people living and renting there about the area. A few 'crime is on the rise here' comments are enough to warrant further investigation.

People who live in an area are often aware of the areas that are losing value or becoming a very poor investment. You could miss this vital information because a great deal comes up in a declining area that is hard to turn down.

When this happens, you just need to remind yourself that if the area is getting worse—then no amount of discount will make investing there a good deal. When you become a keen investigator and begin to pick apart each area, weighing up its good points and bad points, you will learn a valuable skill that you can improve with time.

Eventually, you will be able to go into an area and quickly uncover the truth there. From that starting point, you will see the real differences in property and will be able to discern a good deal from a great one.

A really great deal in a brilliant location might give you equity growth in the future, but it's most important to know how much profitable cash-flow you can make right now. This is where the rental yield comes in. Remember cash-flow is what you want!

Research into locations can take some time, and while some areas may seem to have potential on the face of it, you will not really know until you have fully investigated it further using the techniques suggested here.

If the area that you are interested in will not provide you with adequate profitable cash-flow from the rental income, it's not a good investment. Look elsewhere because there are great locations everywhere.

Examples of Where to Buy

The two basic financial criteria for any good property investment are that it needs to pay for itself and it needs to pay you cash-flow on a monthly basis. You need to decide realistically how much income you need each property investment to generate for you each month. Once you know that these two criteria are fixed, they eliminate a lot of decisions for you.

Simply put—if the property does not meet your financial criteria then ditch it. There are plenty more out there. Now, Britain is an excellent place to begin investing in property because we are at the low point in the property price cycle, as outlined earlier, and there is rising demand to rent properties because the majority can no longer afford to buy, or don't want to own, their own home. Many countries share these property characteristics where there are a glut of cheap properties for sale that can be refurbished to raise their value and then rented out to pay you a passive income.

Here's a UK example of what to be aware of. Recently the Stoke-on-Trent City Council decided to sell run-down homes in Stoke for £1, as part of an area-wide urban renewal program. Wow, only £1, you may think. The price is so cheap that it cannot be a bad investment right? Wrong!

Although the properties are amazingly cheap, buying in this area in Stoke means that you will have to deal with rapidly worsening crime levels, and the threats of squatting, vandalism, burglary, and arson that has plagued the small town. These properties are not habitable in their current condition, which means that you would need to invest tens of thousands of pounds to restore them to a suitable condition. But when you have done that, how easy do you think it would be to rent it out to provide you with a long-term income? Almost impossible because who would want to live there? Certainly not the type of tenant that you need to look after your property for you!

So here are a few tips for you that you should bear in mind when picking your area:

- Only buy in areas that are improving economically and socially.
- Only buy in areas that deliver against your financial criteria.
- Great areas are not always the cheapest; look for the hidden gems that are one or two levels up from the crime hotspots.
- Only invest where there are good local amenities and transport infrastructure.
- Pick areas with local employers and good employment rates.
- Only buy if there are good schools, colleges, or educational facilities.
- Invest where there is a healthy rental market.

The prices and area analysis must add-up. Compare your notes, do not be afraid to explore lots of properties, and you will find the gems and make the right decisions.

I think it is really important to buy locally and where you know. I would advise anyone reading this book to buy in their own country, and ideally in an area that they know. If you do not stick to these two simple rules, it is likely that you will pay the price—namely spending too much time, effort, and money on non-profitable deals.

Let me tell you about an old neighbour of mine called Robert who I met up with in 2011. We had moved away from the town, and I had not seen him in more than ten years. Robert did not stick to the rules and he lost a lot of money.

Robert is in his mid-40s, happily married and a father to Tom and Sarah. After a successful career in the army, Robert set up his own business, worked hard, and became a successful local entrepreneur. He knew that buying properties and renting them out would give him assets that would also provide his family with an additional income stream. With the profits from his business he invested in buy to let property in the UK and in only a few years he had bought 18 houses. Impressive, right?

The problem was that Robert bought them all across the country from Newcastle to Swansea and from Norwich to Portsmouth. He also managed them all himself because he wanted to keep all the profit and did not believe in using letting agents. The result was that he spent much of his spare time driving up and down the motorways of Britain at the beck and call of his tenants. Whenever there was a problem at any of the properties, Robert would jump in his car to sort it out. It took him a long time to find reliable local tradesman for all his properties as they were spread across such a wide area and he often ended up doing any repair work himself. That said, who wouldn't want what Robert had—thousands of pounds of extra monthly income?!

The problem that Robert had created for himself was that he had made a second full-time job and as such there was no way anyone would describe his rental income as 'passive'! He worked long hours on his main business and increasingly every spare moment he had would be spent on his properties.

Robert told me that he had finally had enough when one November morning he was called by one of his tenants in Bristol complaining that the central heating had broken down. Before he got in his car to make the three hour drive, he had promised Tom that he would be back in time for his son's first rugby match that afternoon. Tom was nine years old and was thrilled to have been picked for the school team for the first time, and wanted his Dad on the touchline to give him support.

Robert got down to Bristol in good time, fixed the problem with the heating (it was a simple job of reigniting the boiler's pilot light) and he started to make his way home. Unfortunately there was a huge traffic jam on the M4 motorway caused by a car crash. He was stuck fast and the traffic was hardly moving. Robert was getting increasingly frustrated as the hours went by and the kick-off time for Tom's rugby match was getting closer. Finally Robert had to make a call to Tom to tell him he was not going to make it. Robert said to me, *"I felt sick to my stomach, Jamie, because I had promised him I would be there that morning and had let him down again. I could hear the disappointment in the boy's voice. I had lied to him."*

After that day Robert began to question what he was doing with his property business—what was the point of generating a fantastic second income if he put that ahead of spending time with his young family. He told me that in 2007 he then spent the next two years selling off 12 of the most distant properties so he could concentrate on six that are closer to home. As the Credit Crunch had struck at that time and the economy was sliding into recession, the only people who would buy his properties were other property investors in the local areas, and they wanted heavy discounts. Although Robert sold most of those properties at a slight loss and his rental income took a big hit, he was left with a smaller, local portfolio that he felt was more manageable (he still does not believe in letting agents!) and he could spend more time with his loved ones.

The lesson here is to do the opposite of what Robert and thousands of other investors do, and that is, buy locally. Some of the big property gurus tell you the same thing because you gain from economies of scale and the portfolio is easier to manage, but I advise anyone to go one step further. If you can make higher rental yields, and therefore profits, investing in an area far away from your home, then pick that location and stick to it. This is often beneficial for investors who live in affluent areas where rental yields are low and property prices are high. You will still get the benefits of investing in one concentrated geographical area, but you will need to do more research upfront and find reliable letting agents (more on that later).

Proof the Process Works

At this point, you are probably wondering where the proof is that going through all of this trouble does in fact lead to more accurate and more lucrative property purchases. The proof will come when your portfolio begins to funnel you lots of passive income!

When the money starts coming in, do some of these basic calculations:

Gross Yield: The percentage of your Return on Investment (ROI) each year. To work it out, take your rent per annum and divide it by your purchase price and refurbishment costs.

Example: Property rents at £8400 per year, cost £76,000 to buy and £5000 to refurbish.

Formula: £8400 / £81,000 = 10.3 Gross Yield

Net Yield: Your percentage return on your investment per year, after costs. Gross Yield less costs (maintenance fees, insurance, finance fees, letting fees etc.)

If the costs are 8.5% in this example (which is typical) then it's 10.3% - 8.5% = 1.8%

Your Cash-Flow: The cash-flow here is worked out as the Net Yield of the purchase price and refurbishment costs.

In other words, you cash-flow for this property is 1.8% of £81,000 = £1458 (£121.50 per month)

Apply these calculations to any property situation to determine whether you will make money on the deal or not. ***Here's a top tip—never invest in properties that have less than 8.5% Gross Yield.*** If you do, you won't make any profit.

When you are calculating what your cash-flow or rental yield will be per property, then it has to be part of your overall investment strategy. Location is the prime reason that you will be able to get this kind of yield from your chosen property.

Buy at a high gross yield to get the property that will make you the most money. To do this, use the location skills we have spoken about in the chapter. If you drop the ball on location assessments, expect your Gross Yield to be lower.

The process of finding the best possible area for your property will only work if you are armed with these property calculations. Use these to find yourself viable properties that will continually earn you passive income for years to come.

It is also a good idea to review your properties fairly often. While it is standard practice for rent to increase every year, thereby improving your yield, this can change, so keep informed about what is happening in your local market. Be the Property Ironman, and find property based on solid proof that will earn you income.

Location Selection Case Studies

Case Study 1: Ben Gerstein

Ben Gerstein is a young, up-and-coming property investor friend of mine who became so good at finding the right locations for his properties that he was a millionaire within five years of starting to invest in property.

We cannot all be as freakishly good at this as Ben, but here is his story to inspire you! Ben was 28 when his father passed away and left him a small inheritance that he decided to invest in property.

About two years on, after Ben had bought two retail properties of his own, he began to notice growth in a town in Wales called Caerphilly. The interesting thing about Caerphilly was that the government was building new transport systems there, and it had a great reputation as an historical town among the locals.

Ben did a lot of searches online to find out about the area. He discovered that there was a burgeoning tourist trade here, due to attractions such as Caerphilly Castle and The Big Cheese Festival, which attract people from out of town. Plus the mountain ranges there were becoming more popular as places to bike, climb, and hike.

Ben went to the town to ask around and see what it was like in person. He found that there were many businesses being erected in a specific part of town, probably due to the expansive tourist trade, and the new rail line that was being built there. As a commuter town, leading to both Cardiff and Newport, the potential was great.

After much investigation and number crunching, Ben came across a large retail park that was being sold off at cost. He made his decision and bought several units in that park. Then he bought the land leading out from the park, in case the expansion persisted.

As it turns out, this was a fantastic strategic move, and Ben ended up making a small fortune on his retail investment in Caerphilly. It was the right time, the right place—with a property investor who took the time to locate the specific street and building he wanted.

Ben had no trouble renting out every single unit he bought at that park. With such a sound investment, he more than quadrupled his passive income—which allowed him to refinance and purchase even more properties.

You can argue and say that Ben was lucky, but a Property Ironman knows that preparation, strategy, and proper execution isn't luck—it is skill. Ben has spent the better part of two years learning everything there is to know about property investment, especially where to invest—as this is what drives property value.

His strategy was to invest in stable growth areas, and it paid off for him. While these opportunities do not come along every day—they can happen if you are aware of what's happening in the market and you're keeping your finger on the pulse of the property sector growth patterns—and are willing to do some basic grunt work.

Case Study 2: Julie Hogbin

Another friend of mine is Julie Hogbin, who lives in Bexleyheath in Kent. Julie is new to property investment and only started at the beginning of 2012. She has invested heavily in her property education because she wants to learn as much as possible so she can take action and become financially free.

Julie is also a big fan of going to property networking events because she has learnt so much from her peers. Rather than sit passively, she is one of those people who is not afraid to ask the property speakers questions to improve her knowledge.

She is also an action taker. In less than a year and only with a small amount of money behind her, she now has a property portfolio worth £770,000 with £140,000 equity and that generates her a growing monthly income.

I interviewed Julie recently and one of the most powerful things she said to me was that anyone can become successful in property.

"One of my core beliefs is that people can be what they want to be. We all have a different starting position and some of us are more fortunate than others, but we can all do these things. You don't have to be qualified, or have masses of qualifications, professional qualifications or academic qualifications to operate within the property field." She's right. Anyone can make property work for them if they know what to do.

I think Julie is a real inspiration and proves that you can become a Property Ironman in a very short time if you learn and take action.

If you want to hear more about my interview with Julie you can access it at: **www.thepropertyironman.com**

10 Location Pitfalls during Selection

There are lots of pitfalls that can trip you up if you do not carefully assess your strategic moves when learning which areas to invest in. Here are ten common pitfalls to look out for.

1. *Ignoring your budget*: You may not think so now, but wait until you find an irresistible deal that you can't pass up. That's when it can be tempting to break your budget and offer more for then property than you need. *Property Ironmen* never, ever stray from the budget you have set, for any reason.

2. *Not exploring all of your options*: It is nice to get excited about a certain property or area, but keep in mind that first choices are not always the best choices. The more you look around and gain some context, the better off you will be. Do as much research as you can online, and then ask local experts for their opinions before visiting the area in person. Once you have a 'gut feel' for an area stick with it.

3. *Do not forget to scope the area*: Look for tell-tale signs that your area is what the estate agents or websites say it is. Just because your property might look like it is great value you can't neglect to look out for the potential warning signs and be prepared to walk away. Graffiti-strewn walls, rundown buildings, mattresses left in the street and litter are tell-tale signs.

4. *Do not use emotion when assessing an area*: It is easy to be attracted to an area but only settle on your chosen location if the financials work for you. If they don't, find somewhere else. Ignore this and you could lose a lot of money.

5. *Look at infrastructure*: Infrastructure and access to local amenities helps boost property prices, so you'll want lots of it in your chosen area. A lack of government investment in infrastructure means that the area is not an up-and-comer.

6. *Ignore the rental reality*: Is there much rental demand in your location? Why would someone want to rent your property? If your area cannot answer these simple questions, then renting is going to be an uphill battle—and you want it to be simple. Do not forget that you need the rental yield to give an annual return 8.5% or more.

7. *Do not buy property when the sun is shining*: Unless you live in an area of year-round sunshine, do not buy when it is sunny! Sunshine helps make even the most rundown areas look attractive and local people you pass in the street seem happier. In the UK, for example, this is not the 'norm'. Get a real impression of your potential investing area by doing adequate research and asking lots of questions.

8. *Do not invest in multiple locations:* Do not buy overseas or in a scattergun fashion across various locations. Buy in a concentrated area where you can become a local expert through your research and later from experience. If you want to invest in an area that's far from where you live find reliable estate agents, letting agents and tradesmen—this will save you wasting time and money and creating another job for yourself.

9. *Forgetting about transport*: Transport is easily the most crucial bit of infrastructure in any area. Your potential tenants need to be able to get to work or out to the shops. If your chosen location has poor transport, you'll want to think twice about investing there.

10. *Look at direction and view*: Location is important when buying property—but so is which direction your property faces and whether or not it has a view. These can be strong motivating factors when a tenant is looking to rent from you. One of my friends has a

property next to a high security prison in Leeds and he can't understand why some people don't want to rent it!

The location of your property must be a calculated choice, based on a number of factors that can be measured and used in the decision-making process. Do not forget about these common pitfalls when deciding where to buy your property for an increased shot at success.

Learning from Experience

In property investment, few things are as important as gaining valuable experience from the decisions that you make when investing. A Property Ironman is someone who constantly learns from past experience, and uses it to become a more powerful investor.

Aside from book-knowledge, investing in your education and getting a property mentor, experience is an incredible way to reach the top of your game in the property investment niche. Because you are you, there are certain things you will get right and others that you will get wrong. Some things you naturally like doing and others you don't.

Your first-hand experience will go a long way in preventing you from making the same mistakes twice, and they will help reveal areas in investment that you need to work on. When you do something, that's when you truly understand how it works.

In property investment, if you do something wrong and experience the financial repercussions of that, you are far less likely to repeat that mistake. There is no way you can build your skills and talents without gaining lots of great investment experience.

When you have a process down that works well for you in practice—you will also be better equipped to combine your learned experience with any new, book knowledge or advice that you've received from your peers or a mentor.

I've always viewed my property investment journey as a way to make the most of various talents that I've been given. Little did I know that my weak points would also be highlighted when I began to practice property investment full-time!

Understanding where to buy the best property can only be learned through experience. You need to buy a few great properties and maybe a few bad ones as well. Mark Homer says that the mistake he made buying the ski chalet in Bulgaria was, in hindsight, one of the best things that he did because he learnt from it and is now a multi-millionaire. With each mistake and with every acquisition, you will continually build on that sound knowledge base of experience that will help you become more of a success as time goes by.

There is a reason why the older you get, the fewer mistakes you make in business. This personal experience is reserved only for those that want to really make a huge impact in their property investment careers.

It is a well-known fact that people with lots of practical experience are more effective at what they do. To reach this stage in your career, when you no longer have to work as hard for answers—when a simple gut-feeling based on experience will guide your decisions, that is where you want to be.

So, I encourage you to do the best that you can. Seek out other property millionaires and learn from them. You will undoubtedly make mistakes but do not fear them. Recognise them, move on quickly, and do not repeat them. It is so easy to forget what we have learned that sometimes we have to learn lessons more than once.

Instead, write down your experiences in a property investment journal. Document your successes, your failures, and your epic learning experiences. That's how you become someone like me—a full blown Property Ironman.

From there, it is just a matter of time before you own a massive property portfolio and never have to work in your life ever again! Let's not get ahead of ourselves.

Remember: Find the best location to locate the best profits

In the following chapter we will move to the next step in the Winning 3PR model—Property: What to Buy.

Step 2: Property – What to Buy

"It's tangible, it's solid, it's beautiful. It's artistic, from my standpoint, and I just love real estate."

DONALD TRUMP

Knowing what to buy when you've never had the personal experience of buying successfully before can be a daunting task. A Property Ironman first takes a hard look at all available information on offer, and then makes a strategic decision, based on the evidence about what type of property to invest in. If you get this second step right then you will be able to create long-term wealth for yourself and your family.

We've already touched on how many people lose focus. So how about you? Do you get easily distracted?

I know that I struggle with this one! There is so much choice when investing in property that it can be confusing to know which direction to turn, and I liken it to going to the shops to buy sweets when we were children.

Imagine you are by my side one Saturday morning in April 1977. I am six years old, and I am walking down the high street to our local sweet shop in Fleet called Ye Olde Tuck Shop. My mum is holding my left hand and in my right I'm clutching a shiny ten pence piece, which was my weekly pocket money. Remember this was a LONG time ago!

It is a sunny day, and I'm quite warm in my purple corduroy trousers and crocheted jumper with the yellow face of the Honey Monster on the front—must have been the height of fashion in the 1970s! All I can think about are what sweets I am going to buy. The sweet shop is quite old, the white paint is slightly peeling off the big bay windows at the front, and when you open the door a bell above chimes to announce your arrival to the owner. Inside is like Nirvana to a young boy!

There are three walls in front and to the sides of us, with glass display counters in front of those, and if I get on my tip-toes I can just about see over the top. On the walls are row upon row of shelves, and on those shelves are dozens of glass bottles filled with sweets of all shapes, sizes, and colours. The sugar-sweet smell in the shop is almost too much to bear; my pulse would quicken, and I'd start salivating immediately. There is almost too much choice in those jars, and I remember regularly getting in trouble for not deciding what to buy quickly enough!

In England in 1977 we had half pence coins, and even at my young age I had worked out that I could buy 20 half penny sweets with my weekly pocket money. The trouble was deciding what to get.

I really liked Fruit Salads and Black Jacks, Flying Saucers and Cola Bottles, Strawberry Bon Bons and Sherbet Fountains, but I always wanted to get the most number of sweets possible and some cost more than others. All this meant I had choices to make —really important choices for a six year old!

Looking back, I almost always went for the Fruit Salads and Black Jacks, but it was still a thrill to spend time in that shop every Saturday morning trying to make up my mind.

Just like Ye Olde Tuck Shop there are loads of different types of property available to invest in these days, and you have a tough choice to make. It is choice that can literally create a profitable asset for life, if you get it right. But like the sweet shop you will have your favourites, and then there will be those properties that look great, but can leave a sour taste in your mouth.

Your Property Buying Guide

In the sport of triathlon there are a wide variety of ways that you can compete. You might want to enter the Half-Ironman race, or only do the Super Sprint, the Sprint, or Olympic distance races. You can race as an individual or as part of a team relay. If you're feeling confident and have trained enough, you could enter a full Ironman race.

Just like in triathlon, you have a large variety of choices when deciding what type of property to invest in. As you know, there is never just one type to choose.

Broadly there are two types of property to invest in: *commercial and residential.*

- Commercial property is designed for business use such as leisure, healthcare, office, industrial, and retail enterprises.
- Residential property provides living accommodation, and it is this type of property investment that the *Property Ironman* will concentrate on.

Here is a brief rundown of the types of properties you could invest in:

- **New Build Property:** As the name suggests, these properties are newly built, which comes with a few great advantages for the buyer. You will not have to spend much on repairs, they often come with 10 year guarantees, and you may be allowed to pick out the fixtures and interior of the home that you buy. On the downside, rooms are often smaller than older homes, and you pay a premium for a brand new home (despite the 'huge' discounts and incentives that the developer might throw in to get the sale).
- **Off-plan Property:** These types of property have not yet been built and are often still in the planning stage. You are literally relying on architectural drawings and glossy brochures to make your purchasing decision. Developers attempt to sell these properties before they begin work on their construction, often selling

in phases to secure funds to generate cash-flow before promoting the next phase. If you get in early you could get the best discounted price. On the other hand, you rarely get a true discount because profits and sales commissions are already factored into an often over-inflated asking price, and a large number of units can be completed at the same time, which can make renting out difficult (as I found out to my cost—more about that later!)

- **Flats:** A flat or 'apartment' is a self-contained housing unit that is part of a complete building. These are often called blocks because they contain many units. Flats can be more affordable than larger properties and can be conveniently located in the centre of towns. However, there are often substantial additional costs involved in owning a flat as they are typically leasehold, with annual ground rent and service charges.

- **Detached or Semi-detached Houses:** A detached house is a freestanding residential building, while the semi-detached house is usually a single building that is built to house two families and the two units are often the mirror image of each other. These properties can be more expensive than flats and terraced houses and are particularly suitable for families or house sharers.

- **Terraced Houses:** These are also called 'linked' houses as they are built in a row and share walls and roofs. These properties are common in the UK, particularly in many northern towns and cities, and can be less expensive to buy, manage, and refurbish than detached or semi-detached houses.

It is vital that before you decide on what type of property to invest in you research what is best in your area. Do not let emotions dictate what you invest in; let the financials make the decision for you. These define your strategy and once chosen, stick to that strategy doggedly. That razor sharp focus will help create the long-term wealth you want.

If you want to invest in flats, for example, check that there is adequate local demand and rental yields are high enough to give you a profitable return. Alternatively if there is more demand by young families to live in semi-detached properties, that should be your focus. Before you decide on a strategy, get as much information as possible from local investors or other property professionals such as letting and estate agents about your area—you might be surprised at what they tell you.

I always invest for cash-flow and I would advise anyone reading this to do the same. My chosen strategy is to invest in two and three-bedroom terraced properties in Leeds. The reason is that rental demand is high, prices are relatively low and yields are great. Any increase in the value of my properties over time is a bonus and it isn't a factor on deciding what type of property I buy because I only invest where I can get profitable monthly cash-flow, from Day 1. On the other hand, if you want capital appreciation over the long-term and do not need the monthly cash-flow now, you might want to consider the more affluent areas such as London, Cardiff, Aberdeen, or Edinburgh for example.

Buying Now vs. Buying Before

Since 1990, the UK has experienced a severe drop in housing affordability for anyone wanting to invest in property. Since then, house prices have risen faster than job earnings—which have lagged behind.

To give you a better idea of how house prices have progressed since then, you can refer to *Table 1*.

Year	All Houses		New Houses		Modern Houses		Older Houses	
1990	£ 54 919	-10.7	£ 64 971	-9.2	£ 55 768	-8.1	£ 49 902	-10.6
1991	£ 53 635	-2.3	£ 63 580	-2.1	£ 54 790	-1.8	£ 49 074	-1.7
1992	£ 50 168	-6.5	£ 61 071	-3.9	£ 51 034	-6.9	£ 45 665	-0.9
1993	£ 51 050	1.8	£ 60 008	-1.7	£ 52 038	2.0	£ 47 183	3.3
1994	£ 52 114	2.1	£ 61 586	2.6	£ 52 703	1.3	£ 47 811	1.3
1995	£ 50 930	-2.3	£ 62 772	1.9	£ 51 545	-2.2	£ 46 801	-2.1
1996	£ 55 169	8.3	£ 70 210	11.8	£ 55 408	7.5	£ 50 520	7.9
1997	£ 61 830	12.1	£ 75 462	7.5	£ 61 443	10.9	£ 57 763	14.3
1998	£ 66 313	7.3	£ 78 804	4.4	£ 65 962	7.4	£ 62 658	8.3
1999	£ 74 938	12.6	£ 86 141	9.3	£ 74 283	12.6	£ 71 149	13.7
2000	£ 81 628	9.4	£ 92 950	7.9	£ 81 580	9.8	£ 78 035	9.7
2001	£ 92 533	13.4	£ 104 462	12.4	£ 92 450	13.3	£ 88 656	13.6
2002	£ 115 940	25.3	£ 125 937	20.6	£ 116 789	26.3	£ 112 528	26.9
2003	£ 133 930	15.5	£ 140 892	11.9	£ 134 302	15.0	£ 130 638	16.1
2004	£ 152 464	13.9	£ 162 451	15.3	£ 152 735	13.7	£ 151 337	15.8
2005	£ 157 387	3.2	£ 166 980	2.8	£ 155 297	1.7	£ 154 193	1.9
2006	£ 172 065	9.3	£ 180 964	8.4	£ 169 066	8.9	£ 170 302	10.4
2007	£ 183 959	6.9	£ 192 268	6.2	£ 171 753	1.6	£ 183 599	7.8
2008	£ 156 828	-14.7	£ 164 457	-14.5	£ 146 512	-14.7	£ 156 217	-14.9
2009	£ 162 116	3.4	£ 164 433	0.0	£ 150 746	2.9	£ 162 602	4.1
2010	£ 162 971	0.5	£ 167 395	1.8	£ 151 840	0.7	£ 162 892	0.2
2011	£ 164 785	1.1	£ 172 707	3.2	£ 152 432	0.4	£ 166 107	2.0
2012	£ 163 910	1.6	£ 172 052	1.1	£ 151 360	-1.8	£ 166 351	-1.5

Table 1: Progression of house prices in the UK

You can see that average house prices have steadily increased since 1990. There have been periods of rapid growth (1999 & 2002) and some short-term falls (1990 & 2008), but despite two recessions in this period, property prices have always risen over the medium to long-term.

The take-aways here are:

1. Average house prices have increased over 199% (including during two recessionary periods).
2. New and modern houses cost more to buy than older houses.
3. During this period new house prices have increased 165%, modern houses 169%, and older houses 232%.

4. Older houses cost less to buy and have shown the largest price increases.

Buying a house today will probably cost you more than the £55,000 that it did in 1990 (although not necessarily if you follow the 3PR framework!), but *Table 1* proves that property fundamentals are robust over the medium to long-term across all standard types of property.

My advice to you is to buy older, more established properties that are in demand by tenants in your chosen area. You can secure great deals now because there is still a lot of economic uncertainty and fear in the wider population that is fanned by the media. Buying now, at the bottom of the property cycle, will help you secure assets that will start to rise in price over the next few years as the cycle moves towards growth once again.

Examples of What to Buy

Emotion is by far the worst enemy of evidence-based property investment. It is the one thing that developers and real estate agents count on to sell you deals that may not give you the yield that you need.

There is a process that you need to go through when you buy any property. This process will ensure that you make the right decision every time. I'm going to use a few examples here so that you can see how much of a difference this process makes to property investment.

Determine Your Financial Criteria

What sort of property can you afford? Will this property give you the kind of yield that you need to start building your property portfolio and passive income stream? Most novice property investors buy emotionally instead of thinking about what the long term goal is. The Property Ironman understands where he (or she) is going, and how to get there.

If you need an 8.5% yield, for example, you can only buy a property that meets these financial requirements. In 2005, I was a novice investor that made all the classic mistakes! I bought a two bedroom new build flat in Nottingham that looked very sleek and minimalist in the brochure. I did not do enough research on the area and relied on the developer's assurances that I was buying at a great discount and that the rental yield would make me a healthy monthly profit. After completion, the reality was that it took more than six months to find a tenant because dozens of flats in the same block were available at the same time and we were all competing with each other. This actually forced the rental prices DOWN! In hindsight, I learnt that I had bought badly, or a 'dud', and the rental yield has never been enough to make me any profit over the last seven years.

After educating myself and learning from my initial mistakes, I now only invest in solid terraced houses that meet my minimum rental yield criteria of 10%. Investing in property is not about buying pretty, interesting, or cheap properties and then figuring out how to rent them afterwards.

Property Ironmen know that to build long-term profitable income, you must focus on how much rental yield is achievable with every property you buy. Always buy within your financial criteria and you will find that your wealth grows according to your plan. Technically, there is no step two or three if you get this one right. The financial criteria come first.

When you are looking at what to buy, always aim for the 'ugly' properties with superficial faults that will put the majority of investors off and make it easier for you to buy them at a big discount. Find the faults of the property, tell the estate agent or home owner about them and calculate what they will cost you to put right. Using this tactic will help you to secure property deals at 20% discounts or better. Do you like the sound of that?

Proof the Process Works

A Property Ironman would scrutinise every part of a potential investment property for one solid reason—anything, absolutely anything that can cost you money will decrease your monthly profit.

Being thorough when you check out what to buy can save you thousands of pounds down the track. You'll want to spend a bit of cash on renovating the property so you can increase its value and get a good rental price for it.

When people ask me for proof that my property investment processes work, I will happily show them photos of my properties and the financial spreadsheets, but what is most effective is putting them in touch with friends and clients who I've helped buy property using the 3PR framework. They can express their thoughts better than I ever could on how they have benefited personally from investing in property, and what difference it has made to their lives.

If you would like to contact any of my clients to find out about their success, please email me at: **Jamie@thepropertyironman.com**

Winning Property Case Study

Case Study 1: Shirley Basset

Shirley Basset is a 46 year old woman from Kent who invested £86,000 on her first property investment. When I asked her how she managed to get the money together she said, 'I downsized because I was tired of not having any money.' Shirley had sold her home of 25 years in Maidstone and had moved into a smaller one.

She combined this left over money with a policy that she had cashed out, that was just sitting there being stagnant and not making her any money. The challenge for Shirley was that she knew very little about which properties she should buy.

Shirley sat down with her husband Greg and worked out that they needed a 7% rent yield to get going. Shirley and Greg looked around for a long time, almost investing in a new housing development that was going up near to where they lived. The sales agents raved about the returns, but had no data to back up their claims.

Instead of investing there, Shirley found an older two bedroom semi-detached home that she liked because of its great price and potential. On further investigation and costing, Shirley discovered that she could turn it into a palace with a small £3,400 investment. She made sure that everything was checked out before she bought the property.

As it turns out, there was an insulation problem that was not spotted and the ceiling had to be replaced. She renegotiated the cost with the vendor who took it off the purchase price of the house. Shirley then got to work, replacing the carpets with tiles, updating the fixtures and adding in special extras—such as twin basins in the main bathroom.

When she was finished, she was able to increase the rental yield to a respectable 8%, which was 1% above her minimum criteria. Shirley advertised the 'new' house and found tenants in a record four hours. The very first people who saw her house decided to take it. It was the right size, the right price, looked great and had charming extras that made it worth renting.

This was no mistake—Shirley had simply applied the 3PR buying technique, and had instantly set up her first passive income stream. From there, she refinanced her own home and bought a second place a few months later. Some three years later, Shirley has five investment properties all earning her a healthy passive income.

Property	Proven return	Problems	Additional costs	Extras
The first 'new' home they saw.	5% Rental Yield.	Poor security, many break-ins.	High refuse, water and electricity	None.
The older semi-de-tached home.	8% Rental Yield.	Insulation that lowered the cost of the house.	None.	New fittings, floors, and garden.

Case Study 2: Simon Zutshi

Simon Zutshi is a friend of mind and one of the most highly respected property investors and property educators in the UK. I interviewed him recently and found out that Simon started investing in 1995 when he bought his first home in Birmingham. At the time he was a graduate trainee at Cadbury's and bought a Victorian terraced house near to where he worked. By renting out some of the rooms to friends, he realised that his mortgage and other bills were covered by the rent and he still had some cash left over every month - and this was before he got paid for his day job!

Over a few years he replicated that strategy, by buying similar types of property and rented them out to students as they were all close to the university. As their value rose, he raised additional capital by refinancing his properties so could buy more. Today Simon has a very impressive portfolio of more than 29 properties that are worth more than £6 million and that generates over £7,000 net income per month. This is true passive income as all his properties are managed by letting agents, and all he does is check his bank balance every month.

Simon believes that when many people say they want to replace their income by investing in property, they think they need hundreds of them to do so, but this isn't the case. He argues that most people could replace their income if they bought between four and six properties, "*If* they buy the right kind of properties".

If you want to hear more about my interview with Simon you can access it at: **www.thepropertyironman.com**

10 Pitfalls during the Race

As you can imagine, buying a new property comes with a lot of pitfalls. Just like your first real Ironman event, you can plan all you like but you have to do it to really experience it. Fortunately, I have discovered some very common pitfalls that you can avoid, right from the very beginning.

- *You are looking for a long-term, stable asset, so do your homework.* Work out the relative price rises of different types of property in your chosen area over 10-20 years. Then ask local letting agents or fellow property investors what type of property is most in demand by tenants. This gives you an element of certainty that your property will rise in value and generate a good income over the long-term. Failing to do this could cost you.
- *Define your buying criteria and stick to it!* Work out what type of property you can afford to buy that will also give you +8.5% rental yield. These are your new

buying rules, so if you break these you might regret it.

- *Beware new build and off-plan properties.* Prices are often over inflated, and if you are buying flats they can be difficult to rent out if they all come on to the market together.

- *Rental yields will rise over time, but check the rates quoted by letting agents.* Some letting agents may increase the amount of rent they tell you to expect to win your business, but double check this before buying. Call three local letting agents and compare their rent estimates with those on property portals such as Rightmove. Then post a 'dummy' advert of your potential deal on Gumtree or Easyroommate. com and wait for the enquiries to come in. You will quickly find out what people are prepared to pay.

- *Do not be put off 'ugly' properties!* If you view a house that is full of rubbish, has old-fashioned decoration, has a bit of damp or smells bad, don't walk out straight away. The chances are that other people viewing it will do exactly that and it could be difficult for the vendor to sell it. Often these problems are only superficial and can help you secure a great discount from a desperate seller.

- *Remember to ask about hidden costs with leasehold properties.* If you want to buy a flat, for example, find out upfront from the vendor or estate agent what costs need to be included in your financial analysis—ground rent, estate charges, and service charges can wipe out much of your annual profit if they come as a surprise to you.

- *Establishing the real value of a potential deal can be difficult.* Check recent sold prices of similar houses on property portals and on the Land Registry, or failing that pay a small fee to get an online, real-time valuation of the property you are considering. The more you view and monitor property prices in your local area, the better you will naturally become at recognising a good value deal.

- *Do not ignore older, more established properties.* The chances are that a house that is more than 60 years old is solid and will be around for at least another 60. Always check for structural issues, but most older houses were built to last—they can also be better value too.

- *Guessing how much it will cost to improve a property is a mistake.* If you think you've found a property with great potential, get three tradesmen to quote for any repairs or improvements that will be needed if you go ahead with the purchase. Knowing how much you will need to pay upfront and including these costs in your analysis helps determine not only what price to offer but also the potential profit in the deal.

- *Research but do not over analyse.* It is always vital that you do enough research to answer most of your questions and allay your fears about which properties are right for you. But do not miss out on great deals by procrastinating. If you've done your research but still are worried, trust you gut instinct—it is often right. If you want to become a Property Ironman you have to take action!

Trust Your Training

During the process of selecting a property to buy, one thing always pops into my head. 'Trust your training.' It is the same thing that I think about when I'm swimming those miles in the Ironman competition, trying to reach the opposite shore.

When you have worked out your strategy and have done all the training you need to perfect your swim stroke, you are in a position where you feel relatively comfortable about what you're trying to achieve. The rest is really up to you. I am not saying that bad decisions are impossible to make if you have received the right training; I am just saying they are less likely.

Training to become a great Property Ironman means understanding what to buy down to the micro details. You'll learn a lot from my book and from any worthy property mentor who you find in your local area.

Sometimes a mentor can be a personality in a book (such as Donald Trump or Robert Kiyosaki) or it can be a person you know who has succeeded with property in their lives (such as Simon Zutshi). I cannot stress enough how important I think it is to continue learning as an up and coming Property Ironman.

You can learn in three core ways: from investigation, from a mentor, and through experience. You will need to utilise and leverage all three modes of learning if you're going to become successful.

The next time you see a property deal that you are just not sure about, reread the relevant section of this book or ask your property mentor to check your analysis. A reminder of what to do or an informed second opinion gives you confidence.

Sometimes you might lose money when buying property, but often it is because of something that is outside of your control. The key is to learn from that experience quickly and move on. As John C. Maxwell says, 'fail forward'.
You have already begun your property learning journey by

buying this book. Now, find yourself a mentor who will help you through the details of buying and renting out property. This mentor needs to be highly experienced in the art and science of property investment and have tangible evidence that he or she has succeeded financially with property too.

Often, people choose friends as mentors—which does not work. They have opinions to offer, but you need someone who is impartial and has 'been there, done that,' so that they can share their practical knowledge with you.

Trust the training that you get from all the different sources of knowledge that you acquire on your property journey. Always take this knowledge and make it your own, by changing and applying it to your own life.

Above all remember to focus on the right property today to achieve financial freedom tomorrow.

Let's now look at the next step in the Winning 3PR framework—Pro Team: Your Power Pro Team.

Step 3: Pro Team - Your Power Pro Team

CHAPTER 05

"Talent wins games, but teamwork and intelligence win championships."

MICHAEL JORDAN

The third step in the *Property Ironman* Winning 3PR Framework is the final 'P'—Power Pro Team. If you get this next step right, it can truly accelerate your success. When people ask me how I managed to achieve so much in such a short amount of time, I always say, 'I had help!' What I mean by this is that I have a professional team that advises me, supports me, and provides the added skill sets and expertise that I lack.

When you have learned where and what to buy, the next step is the HOW. And believe me, the 'how' can be treacherous if you are out there alone, trying to make sense of a market that constantly changes.

Building Your Pro Team

It is very important to build a professional team of people who will stand by you and work with you through your property investment journey. I have met a few people who have managed to become property millionaires all on their own, but not many. It is hard work, it can be lonely and it is very boring!

Wouldn't you prefer for others to work hard on your behalf, so you do not have to?

This is the very essence of 'leverage' and if you learn how to do this effectively you save time, save money, and save effort. Sounds better than creating another full-time job to me!

Successful Property Ironmen are supported by a team of people. In Ironman triathlons, it is always the athlete who is seen swimming in the lake, cycling up mountains, or running to the finish by him or herself. It looks like a sport for individuals, and no matter how much we want to say "I did that all by myself", it simply isn't true!

I would never have been able to complete my last Ironman race without the support of my family, friends, coaches, nutritionist, and physio. From my close friend Bernie, who crossed the line with me, to my triathlon coach who helped me improve my swimming and cycling technique—they are all invaluable. Yes, I know we put the actual effort in one the day of the race, but it has taken months of work to get to the start line and no athlete does it alone.

And that is exactly what property investment is like too. If you try and do it alone, you might do okay, but the chances are that you will get disillusioned before long and want to give up. Worse is that you could lose a lot of money. Property investing is technical, and you need specialists to help and guide you. My advice is that it is too hard to win in this game on your own, so take the easier path to success.

The good news is that once you actually start investing, you will naturally build up your own specialist team out of necessity.

At this stage, you will want to find an array of talent, so here is a list of the *minimum* people you need to be in your Power Pro team.

- *Property mentor*: Find a successful property investor who is several levels up from you and is willing to help you on your way. This person should be financially free and highly experienced with a wealth of knowledge to offer.
- *Lawyer or solicitor*: Find a reliable solicitor who specialises in property investment. As well as covering basic conveyancing, you might need them to help you with deeds of trust, creating joint venture agreements, and wills.
- *Financial advisor and mortgage broker*: Choose to

include a sound financial advisor on your team so that you will be aware of what is going on with your finances at all times. You will be able to better envisage your long and short-term financial strategies and stay on the right financial path. Often financial advisors are mortgage brokers too, and as long as they have access to the whole of the market, they will be able to find you the best lending products that suit your needs. If they know your strategy and long-term goals, then they will be able to advise on refinancing and leveraging your portfolio in a responsible way.

- *Accountant*: Many novices forget about tax when buying and renting property, so having a good accountant on your side is key. Ideally, they should be a property investor too so they know the most up to date rules and regulations that you need to abide by.

- *Estate agent*: I know some of you think I have used an expletive here, but estate agents can be your best friends! Poor old estate agents are in one of the most loathed and distrusted professions in the U.K., but times are changing and standards are improving (with many of them anyway). Estate agents who are strategically placed in your investment area can be your eyes and ears on the ground and can source you the best deals. They are also expert negotiators, so get them to work on deals for you.

- *Letting agent:* If you don't want to have to deal with regular issues that arise from being a landlord, you will need a letting agent to manage your property. They can find you suitable tenants, collect the rent, remind you when the annual checks need to be done, evict problem tenants, and sort out minor repairs.

- *Tradesmen:* Unless you want to do any refurbishments yourself, you need to build a team of specialist tradesmen to add value to your property cost-effectively. In addition, having a collection of trusted experts who can deal with any minor problems in your property as soon as they arise will keep your tenants happy so they are likely to stay in your property for longer.

- *Joint Venture Partners:* Unless you are as rich as Midas, or Richard Branson, property investors soon realise that their capital does not last long. You might want to attract other investors or joint venture partners to fund your property purchases. Using other people's money (OPM) can be a great way to accelerate your long-term wealth as well as delivering great returns to your JV investor.

This list can be expanded upon if you need more help—surveyors, cleaners, bank lending managers, and business partners are a just few other suggestions. Decide what your team really needs from the outset and then find the best people to help you reach your goal.

Your Power Pro team must focus on the financial and physical aspects of buying and renting your properties. Each of these members needs to be honest, reliable, trustworthy, and focused on you.

So where do you find your Power Pro Team?

- *Mentors:* As discussed before, you can be mentored by those who write books and produce audio programmes, but I find the most effective way of learning is being mentored my someone who will spend time with you face-to-face. Local property networking events are often a great source of finding mentors. Interview them and find out as much as you can about what they have achieved. Remember that there are many different property strategies out there, so find a mentor who has followed the single-let route (buy/refurbish/rent/refinance model). In my experience, the fees mentors charge are worth at least ten times the value you get back from them.

- *Solicitor, financial adviser & accountant:* These three groups are so important to your financial success over the long-term that I advise everyone to go on recommendation only. Ask your mentor or fellow property investors at networking events and property forums. When you find some companies you think you want to work with, meet them and discuss your requirements and their relative experience to get a feel if they are right for you.

- *Estate agent & letting agent:* Unless you can get a recommendation from a local property investor, the best way I find to recruit estate agents on to your team is to meet as many as you can. Start by visiting a range of nationwide chains and independents and explain that you are a property investor wanting to find out the best places to buy in the area. Get as much information from them that you can and then start viewing properties. You need to view at least 15 properties per month if you want to build rapport with the agent and show that you are serious. Having a mortgage decision in principle helps prove that you have the funds to invest and will not be wasting their time. The same can be said for letting agents. If you can't get any local recommendations, visit as many as you can yourself and find out all you can about tenant demand and prices in your area. If the letting agent is also a property investor then so much the better because they will know exactly what you expect from them as a client.

- *Surveyors:* Your mortgage broker might recommend a local surveyor or you can contact the Royal Institute of Chartered Surveyors (www.rics.org/uk). RICS surveyors have a range of services that can help value any property or identify structural issues before you purchase it. They are also useful when refinancing your property by advising what it is worth after you have added value with the refurbishment.

- *Tradesmen:* Builders, plumbers, certified electricians, and gas engineers can either be found from personal recommendations or from independent websites such as RatedPeople.com, Checkatrade.com, and Toptradespeople.co.uk. These sites enable you to search for good ratings and reviews from pervious customers in your local area who have used them. Letting agents often know reliable refurbishment teams, so ask them too.

- *JV Partners:* There are many places where you can find potential JV investors, so I will list a few to get you started. Friends and family, property networking events, business networking lunches, online property forums, charity balls, business angel events, wealth and lifestyle conferences, flying clubs, sailing schools, golf clubs, business angel events, etc. The key is to talk to as many people as possible, tell them what you do, and if they are interested to find out more, ask them what they want from a potential joint venture first. You will need some property investing experience to be taken seriously, so I always advise that you use your own funds first, become an expert in your chosen area and strategy, and then look for potential partners.

Creating your Power Pro Team means you will always have someone available to answer any questions that crop up, and this in turn will enable you to deal with property issues quickly and with confidence.

It can time take to get every role in your team filled with great people. Some will perform well, and others will let you down. Just remember that your money and dreams are at stake, so if one member of your team is not supporting you adequately, you need to find a replacement quickly. Over time and with some experience, you will find a team that gels and delivers exactly what you want. Persevere because it is worth the effort.

Individual vs. Team Based Success

Building a property investment team is one of the greatest assets you will ever have in your pursuit of success and financial freedom. When you compare individual performance in property investment to team based success, you begin to see the radical differences.

When you are starting out in property investment, you probably won't know much and you might be tentative. Your lack of experience might cause you to lose your initial funds or stop you making any purchases, therefore missing some great deals. Either can cripple you financially. To reduce this risk, let the experts advise you.

A great Power Pro team helps to keep you focused on your goals and on what's important. It is easy to get distracted when you're on your own, and that's when bad decisions are made. I will never forget that first off-plan property I bought in Nottingham. I had read a few property books and my newspaper regularly wrote about the benefits of buy to let investing, but in essence I didn't have a clue! As

I did not have any independent expert advisors to help me, my limited knowledge, desire to make money, and faith in the developer's sales patter meant I lost a serious amount of money—on my very first deal. Ouch! I don't want you to make the same mistake I did.

Individual property investment does take a lot of work, time, and energy. You can succeed on your own, but I believe that taking this path defeats the whole 'personal freedom' aspect that passive property income can give you.

In my several years as a Property Ironman, my team has been a huge factor in my wealth and success. I am 100% convinced that you will also need a Power Pro team on your side if you're going to succeed too.

Proof the Power Pro Team Works

Do you know someone who has bought a property for themselves to live in or as an investment who has lost money? I'm sure we all do, I have even told you about my own mistake!

I relate the complexities of buying property to owning a car. You might drive a car that gives you all the benefits you need—safety, efficiency, reliability, status, convenience. But do you have any idea how to fix the fuel pump if it breaks? Some people do, but most do not. The point is that it does not matter because you know you can ask an expert, such as a mechanic, to do it for you. This might cost you a small amount of money, but the chances are that you will be back on the road in no time.

As an intelligent person you know that investing in property to make passive income is a complex process, so you might as well ask the property experts for help. Henry Ford once said that he didn't have all the answers, but he knew where to find them!

It is easier to see how valuable teamwork is in an Ironman race. Three athletes might enter the race as a relay, each person competing in the one discipline at which they excel. One will swim; the second will cycle, and the third will run. They get the right nutrition to give them energy during the race from sports bars and drinks, and there is a support team who are ready to fix any mechanical problems with the bike or give a massage to aching limbs. If one competitor begins to tire, the other two will give encouragement to keep going. You see this level of teamwork in many triathlons, and it is truly inspiring.

Teamwork does not make you a property millionaire by itself, but it does keep you on the right track to becoming one if you are dedicated. Your Power Pro team will work hard to make sure that you are ahead, and making the right decisions that will positively affect your bottom line.

That is all the proof you will ever need. But don't forget, if things go wrong and one of your team members is not working out, get rid of him! Fortune only favours the brave—and part of being brave is building and maintaining a quality, expert team.

Power Pro Team Case Study: *Roy Inman*

Let me tell you about a friend of mine called Roy Inman who readily acknowledges that his Power Pro Team have been instrumental in helping him build a property portfolio worth more than £6 million pounds, with £1.5 million in equity and a monthly income of £10,000. Do you think you can learn something from Roy?

Roy started out as a chef and worked more than 50 hours each week for a salary of £11,000 per year. At the age of 21 he had saved up £2,000, and by combining that with a personal loan of £15,000, and his father's redundancy payment of £15,000, he was able to buy his first house.

As he didn't have much money, didn't know any better, and is a self-confessed control freak(!), Roy renovated the house by himself. He admits that he did a lot of unnecessary work in the refurbishment, which cost £8,000 and took five months to complete the project. In hindsight, he knows he should have let the experts do it for him - it would have been completed in six weeks and only cost £3,500. Roy was a fast learner and did not repeat that mistake again.

Roy firmly believes that having a good Power Pro Team is priceless for his business.

"It makes things ten times easier, especially if you've got good quality people you can trust. Whether it's people that you employ, or you outsource to, or just joint-venture with, it's invaluable. It means that you can get more done in a shorter space of time; it means that you can bring in other expertise that you don't have to learn. So from that point of view you're gaining knowledge and experience in areas that you wouldn't be able to achieve in a lifetime."

Roy talks a lot of sense and I have learned so much from his no-nonsense approach. If you would like to get my full interview with Roy you can access it at: **www.thepropertyironman.com**

10 Power Pro Team Pitfalls on the Course

Your Power Pro Team will sometimes make some mistakes when you're out there trying to finish the race. But as long as you steer clear of these common pitfalls, you should be alright.

> *1. Do not let one voice overpower the others.* Take all of your team member's opinions into account and don't just choose one particular voice to heed. You will have

to make up your mind, but don't be biased when listening.

2. *If one team member is not performing, fire him or her.* Property investment is about making money—if a team member loses you money, get rid of him or her. You can't afford to keep someone like that on your team.

3. *Not listening to your financial advisor.* Accumulating wealth and building a passive income is what we all want—so listen to your financial advisor. If he or she says you cannot afford something, then you cannot afford it. Do not take unnecessary financial risks.

4. *Do not go against the advice of your mentor.* You pay a mentor for his or her experience and to help accelerate your success. Do not go against the advice. Their reputation is important to them and they want you to reach your goals too. If you are happy with the help you have received from your mentor, then your testimonial is powerful proof for other potential clients.

5. *Becoming reliant on your team.* It is fine to rely on your team up to a point, but you should be aware of getting value from them at all times. If prices start creeping up as you become more successful, make sure they are justified. Do not become complacent with your team.

6. *If your team cannot offer you a solution, find someone who can.* Strategies, rules, and regulations change often in property, so always make sure you are getting the best advice from your team. Network with other investors as they might be using a solution you need, but that your team was not aware of.

7. *Failing to say no to any financial opportunities.* When

your portfolio grows and the cash-flow improves, it is easy to become caught up in buying more and more property. Always refuse deals if they do not comply with your buying criteria. Just wait for the next great deal.

8. *Being afraid of risk.* In property investment it is your financial advisor, accountant, and solicitor's job to help minimise your risk. When starting out, don't let fear of making a mistake stifle you. If you see a great opportunity, run it past them and then go for it.

9. *Do not be tempted to take some refurbishment work on yourself.* When you have developed a great refurbishment team who you trust, do not start taking over smaller jobs to save money or to 'get your hands dirty.' You will make them feel you are checking up on them, take longer to complete it, and probably do a worse job than your team would do. Trust them to get on with the project and spend your time on something more profitable.

10. *Treat your team members well.* Maintain good relations with your team and your wealth and success will flourish with their help. Treating them badly and not paying them what they are worth could lead to dissent and poor decision-making. You do not want to be left high and dry in the middle of a project.

Importance of Team Advice and Shared Expertise

In order for a team to function together effectively, you will need to step up as the leader. That means clearly articulating what each team members duties are, what your goals are, and which project you're working on next.

Team advice and expertise are so crucial to a successful property portfolio that even losing one dynamic team member could affect your bottom line. These people contribute to your success by sharing their knowledge and expertise, so listen to what they say and value their involvement.

Shared advice and expertise means:

- A 360 degree view of a potential property deal
- New perspectives that could bring positives (and negatives) to light
- Enough knowledge to see an opportunity to create a better return
- Confidence that your business is being handled well
- The ability to effectively manage your money
- The ability to take advantage of laws and taxes
- Higher quality refurbishments
- Refurbishments that are a lot more cost-effective
- Opportunity to learn from all of your team members

That final stretch that you run before you finish the Ironman race is really when your training and team progress show. When you are tired and have nothing left to give—that is when you push on. Your team inspires and motivates you to do better. It is one of their most endearing and beneficial features.

You might occasionally make a bad investment decision, but with the collective knowledge of the right team behind you, they could change a financial drain into a financial gain. It is when you work alone that you become demotivated, stressed, and tired. Plus, when you work alone, you will not always know where you have gone wrong.

When you have a dynamic team around you, there is always someone looking out for you. That alone is enough reason to build a quality, intelligent team of property investment professionals.

So do not think that you can achieve financial freedom on your own. Instead, dedicate some time to building a great Power Pro team.

Remember to let the experts work hard for you, so you do not have to work hard.

We are now halfway through the Winning 3PR framework, so let's move on to the first 'R'—Refurbish: Touch Ups and Tricks.

Step 4: Refurbish - Touch Ups and Tricks

"Every day, you'll have opportunities to take chances and to work outside your safety net. Sure, it's a lot easier to stay in your comfort zone...in my case, business suits and real estate... but sometimes you have to take risks. When the risks pay off, that's when you reap the biggest rewards."

DONALD TRUMP

Once you've used the 3Ps to buy the best possible property, it is down to using the 3Rs to get that property turning over a nice income for you on a monthly basis, forever.

I'm going to show you the single biggest thing that **loses** most novice property investors money, so you know how to avoid it! If you get this step right, you will make big profits and you will build a sustainable property portfolio. The very first 'R' stands for Refurbish. Done the right way, refurbishing not only adds value to your property, but it also makes it a desirable place to live in and your tenants will not want to leave.

Have you watched those do it yourself or home improvement television shows? You know the ones— *Property Ladder*, *Homes Under the Hammer* or *Restoration Nightmare*? There are hundreds of them these days and some digital channels are devoted to nothing else! I do not know about you, but I find them almost compulsive viewing because I love the moment when the hapless new investor finally realises that they have not made a single penny in profit. Despite their best intentions and spending painstaking hours on the refurbishment, their investment property is often worth EXACTLY the same as when they first bought it!

This is always the moment when my wife and I are sitting on our sofa with a glass of wine, and we are amazed that the poor old soul cannot remember the countless times that the host has warned them not to install a conservatory, a state of the art wet-room or marble worktops in the kitchen because they are just not necessary! The look of incredulity on their faces is almost always exactly the same, before they recover in front of camera and say that they wanted to rent their property out all along and the price doesn't matter. I despair sometimes, it is not as if they were not warned by the expert! But I guess it does make good television.

The simple truth is that you always make your profit in property when you buy (so always buy at a good price), but you can release much of that profit if you get the refurbishment right, and it is really very simple to do that if you just use some common sense.

I want to tell you a cautionary story about a couple I know who unfortunately got their first refurbishment very wrong. If you were sitting beside me in my black VW Passat in November 2009, driving down Windhill in Bishops Stortford, you would be about to witness something that might have shocked and saddened you.

I pulled up onto the driveway of a red-brick 1930s townhouse in a quiet road in town. The driveway was edged by established plants, and the manicured lawn still had a hint of frost on the ground where the winter sun had not yet reached. On the porch were the two people I had come to meet, Charles and Diana Morgan. They were family friends and were the nicest couple you'd ever want to meet. Diana was in her early 50s, 5 foot 3 inches tall and immaculately but simply dressed in a wool suit and mother of pearl necklace. Charles was in his late 50s, 5 foot 10 inches tall and wearing his habitual shirt and tie. Charles and Diana, an attractive couple, are parents to two boys, Ben and Tom, 18 and 21 years old respectively.

After more than 30 years working in the insurance industry in London, Charlie had been made redundant and with his payout had bought and renovated the couple's first investment property. After a successful career, Charlie knew that they needed to supplement their now meagre income, as Diana only worked part-time doing the book-keeping for a small local publishing company. Charlie was a proud man, and it was his wife who had called me that day to ask for some advice.

Over coffee they began to tell me what had happened to them over the last seven months. They had found and bought a large three bedroom house in Bishop's Stortford, just round the corner from where they lived. Charlie had walked passed the house every day on his way to the train station; it was in a quiet road, close to the centre of town but had begun to look neglected from the outside. It had been on the market for a few months when they had viewed it one Saturday morning, and they found that the inside had also seen better days. The vendor was an elderly lady in her late 70s who could no longer care for herself, so had moved into a nursing home, and her family needed to sell the house to pay for the fees.

Inside the house looked like something out of the 1950s. It had not been decorated for decades, and the faded wallpaper, yellowing paintwork, worn carpets, and Formica kitchen gave the house a tired look. Charlie and Diana had correctly realised that it only needed a superficial refurbishment just to bring the house up to date. They paid £274,000 for the house and planned to rent it to a young family for £1,000 per month. I did a quick calculation and worked out that this would give a rental yield of just over 4% and they would probably not make a single penny in profit—it was definitely a deal I would have run away from!

Diana offered me a biscuit and said, *"That was when our problems really started."* Charlie saw the refurb project as a chance to work with Diana for the first time. She had an artistic flair that they thought would help make their property really stand out and make it a desirable place to live for future tenants. The couple had given themselves a budget of £15,000 to refurbish the house, which they thought was adequate to make it a 'dream' family home, and indeed it should have been.

Unfortunately, the costs started spiralling out of control and their enthusiasm and inexperience, caused them to make bad decision after bad decision. The Formica was replaced with a sleek modern kitchen, a new range cooker was added together with the (infamous) marble worktops, the bathroom was updated with a power shower and Jacuzzi bath, and wooden floors were laid throughout. The project was finished to a very high standard, and I asked them how much they had spent. *"We think it's just under £26,000,"* said Charlie.

I could not believe that they had spent a whopping 170% more than their budget! They had made the classic mistake of improving the house to a standard that *they* would want if they moved in, without bearing in mind what they *needed* to do to make it a suitable rental property for their target tenants. The result was a massive overspend and a huge waste of money.

What made matters worse is that they had finally gone through their finances and realised that the rent they could charge would not even cover their costs, so they would need to use more of their savings to pay for the bills and management charges for the house. Despite their best intentions, their first investment property had used up most of their savings and at the same time would not generate the income they needed. With Tom at university and Ben planning to go next September, they needed some extra money very quickly.

As a friend of theirs, the saddest part for me was sitting opposite Charlie at the kitchen table and seeing how the stress and worry had made him look so much older. After a very successful career in the city with the status and lifestyle that comes with that, here he was a few months later miserable, full of doubt and regret.

Later that morning we visiting the house and by looking at the room layout, I advised them to rent the bedrooms out on an individual basis to young professionals on a house-share basis. This isn't suitable for everyone, but because the town is close to Stansted airport and a major commuting area for London, I knew there was good demand from these types of tenants. By turning the dining room into an extra bedroom, Charlie and Diana were then able to rent out their four bedroom house at £450 per room per month, including bills. Although they invested £95,000 into this property (deposit, refurbishment costs, legal fees) and will probably not be able to access any of that unless the market prices improve over the next few years, they at least were able to make over £630 net profit each month from the rent. This additional income helps support their lifestyle and pays some of their son's living expenses at university.

I hope this story helps illustrate the main points to bear in mind if you want to increase your profits through careful refurbishing. Remember to keep your emotions out of all decisions, have the tenants' requirements in mind when doing the work, and above all use some common sense!

Old vs. New Refurbishment Rules

Twenty years ago, it was enough to slap on some paint and tidy things up a bit in order to successfully rent a property. Rogue landlords treated their tenants badly; many kept their rent deposit monies (or 'bond') and provided sub-standard housing. If they dared complain about the conditions they lived in, they were often removed from the property and a replacement tenant was found! These days 'Generation Rent' requires better standards, and landlords also have a duty of care to provide safe and secure accommodation, as well as treat their tenants fairly. The property laws in many countries have also been updated to protect the rights of both the landlord and tenants in a more equitable way, and it is vital that you know what is required of you as a landlord. If you do not, you are open to legal action being taken against you.

That said, it is wise to have a great letting agency as part of your Power Pro team to act on your behalf who can advise you on your responsibilities so you don't have to know all the ins and outs of the law.

Here are a few refurbishment tips that will keep your tenants safe and give you peace of mind:

- All appliances that you add must have a gas safety certificate.
- Gas safety checks should be made annually by a certified expert (e.g. CORGI engineer).
- Carbon monoxide detectors near every gas appliance in your property may not be compulsory, but they are inexpensive and can save lives.
- All electrical equipment needs to be checked regularly and should have the CE marking in Europe (the manufacturer's statement that it meets all legal standards).
- The fitting and supply of fire doors, hard-wired fire and smoke alarms, extinguishers and fire blankets are all advisable.
- If you are furnishing your property, upholstered furniture needs to be fire resistant.

Rules change, and many local authorities have different landlord requirements so it is advisable to ask your letting agent or council housing department to find out what you need to do.

When I refurbish properties in Leeds I want to do them to a standard that is above the minimum required by the local authority so that I can almost future-proof them for a period of time. It gives me peace of mind that should any accident happen, I know that I have done all I can to protect my tenants (and my property). This helps ensure that my tenants and I have a great relationship based on trust, and they are more likely to stay in my houses, but more on that in the next chapter!

Inevitably, you have to do what is best for your property. Make it look good, make it safe, and you will have no problems renting it out and raising its value.

There are parallels with competing in Ironman triathlons too. Doing a good refurbishment and improving the safety features in your property is similar to doing all the basic fitness training, stretching, and getting the right nutrition for Ironman. You cannot necessarily see all the improvements, but you have safeguarded yourself against many of the smaller things that can go wrong. You don't want anything breaking or dropping off do you?! Doing the basics right will help you keep your tenants longer, which is similar to being able to stay in the race until you cross the finish line.

Your Touch Up Tricks

There are so many ways to add *appropriate* value to your properties when refurbishing. I use the word appropriate because many of the tips and tricks depend on the strategy or area that you invest in, but the overall aim for every Property Ironman is to refurbish the property with the target tenant in mind. So, here are a few general rules that I use to get us started.

- Do not get emotional when deciding on what your property will look like when the work has been completed. Always use neutral paint for the walls, white paint for the woodwork and a plain carpet (I find brown and grey work well). Tenants want a home that looks fresh and modern and a simple room with neutral colours is a perfect.

- Controlling your costs is also vital if you want to make a profit. When setting out a budget get three quotes, ideally from recommended tradesman, if this is your first investment property. When you have a budget, get your refurb team to sign off on it. This stops any potential disputes over costs at the end of the project. By getting an agreed 'Bill of Quantities' it becomes your checklist to confirm all works have been finished to an adequate standard. I recommend paying your refurb team in staged payments so that they only get the final amount once you are satisfied that all snagging has been completed. This keeps them accountable to you, and in return you must pay them on time. This is a small thing but many investors don't do this, and it helps to ensure they will do a great job for you each and every time.

- So what is the minimum or maximum that you should spend on a refurbishment? How much is too little or too much? I get asked this a lot. It really does depend on what tenants in your area expect, but the rule of thumb that I use is for every £1 spent on a refurbishment, aim to increase the value of the property by £3. When it comes to replacing kitchens, for example, I don't spend more than £1,700 on a fully-fitted, quality kitchen. This includes tiling and the standard white goods too. Using this rule means that I expect the new kitchen to add at least £6,000 to the overall value of the property. This also demonstrates the importance of having a great refurbishment manager as part of your Power Pro team. They will be able to get trade, or wholesale, prices for all products, which can save you a fortune.

- It is also important not to spend too little, especially when it comes to looking after the safety of your tenants. Meeting or exceeding the minimum safety standards required by your local council means you will comply with your duty of care as a professional landlord, and it doesn't have to cost very much. Fire doors cost £150 each, fire blankets, carbon monoxide detectors, and extinguishers can all be bought on eBay for about £100.

- Using self-employed specialists such as Corgi registered gas engineers, carpet fitters, and electricians can also keep your costs down. I know someone who spent £3,800 re-carpeting their three bedroom investment property using exactly the same manufacturer I use, and yet it only costs me just over £1,000!

One of the often over-looked benefits of buying a property that needs refurbishing is that estate agents will have no idea how much the actual cost of the work will be. They have probably never refurbished a property from a *Property Ironman's* perspective before, so use this to your advantage when negotiating. If you think a refurb will cost you £8,000, tell the estate agent it will cost double that - you might get a great deal!

When my refurb has been finished, I always get a professional cleaning company to come in to give the property a 'sparkle clean'. For about £50 it does exactly what it says on the tin - they make the property look immaculate, and it is amazing that such a little thing can make a big impression on prospective tenants. It amuses me that a clean house can give it a 'wow' factor!

Many investors fail to improve the look of their property from the outside. First impressions can be very important to tenants (and surveyors), so spend some time making the front clean and tidy. If you have a garden replace broken fencing and cut back any wild plants. Repainting the outside of the house can make a dramatic improvement to its appearance, especially for older properties, so if it is within budget, do it.

Although this will vary by region, I normally spend up to £6,000 on a two bedroom and up to £9,000 on a three bedroom refurbishment project. Others spend a lot more, and some a lot less. In my investment area, this is adequate to make my tenants want to move in immediately and for the surveyors to raise the value of my properties.

Proof That Touch Ups Make Profit

I bought a two bedroom stone cottage in one of my investment areas of Leeds in March 2012. The property cost me a bit more than £60,000, and I knew at once that it had great potential. Thankfully, everyone who viewed it before me was put off by the out-dated decoration, worn carpets, dirty kitchen, and black-tiled bathroom! I viewed the property for a second time with my refurbishment manager, and we estimated the cost of works before we left.

There was nothing structurally wrong with the house, and it just needed some minor cosmetic improvements and a good clean. Once the property was mine, the refurb team took a little over two weeks to finish the project, and two weeks later my new tenant moved in.

The refurb cost me a total of £2,600 and a little more than nine months later the same property was re-valued by a local surveyor at £85,000! At a time when house prices in my investment area were stagnant, the refurbishment had impressed the surveyor so much that he had increased the value by more than £20,000. Not a bad return for a bit of effort!

As we saw at the beginning of this this chapter, Donald Trump rightly says, stepping outside of your comfort zone can be risky, and many novice investors view buying properties that need a refurb as taking a big risk. It can feel daunting initially, but I hope that with some of the guidance from this book you can minimise your risks, and once you get a great result like the one above you will 'reap the biggest rewards'.

If you can learn to see the potential in a building and do some basic cost analysis, you will learn to find some real gems that can make you a lot of money.

Like all good Property Ironmen, I've become quite a pro at choosing properties that need work, and then increasing their value and maximising the rental returns. In triathlons small adjustments to technique, slight changes to equipment, and effective training can all combine to amplify your performance on race days.

Refurbishment Case Study: *Gill Alton*

I had the great pleasure of meeting up with a friend of mine recently, Gill Alton, who is a real force of nature!

Gill and her family have been investing in property for 18 years and have built up a portfolio worth £1.66m. This is impressive in its own right, but that portfolio also provides them with a monthly income of £7,600.

Although living in Berkshire, Gill invests in Nottingham where her husband originally comes from. She is an expert at finding good value houses and renovating them to add value. While being a mum, Gill also runs a mentoring business and a property investing business.

She met her refurbishment manager in Nottingham from a recommendation, and since then the partnership has proved a very successful one. To date they have just finished their 34th property!

Gill makes her property investing decisions based on the equity she can create after the refurbishment, and the properties she buys typically give 'net returns' on the cash invested of between 7% - 11%.

She is an incredibly dynamic lady who wants to help as many people as possible benefit from property investing. Her husband is a mortgage broker, and together they worry about how many millions of people have not adequately prepared for their retirement.

Gill believes that only a handful of properties can be the difference between living on the breadline and enjoying your later years to the full. If you would like to get Gill's contact details and access to the rest of our interview you can do so by visiting my website: **www.thepropertyironman.com**

10 Touch Up Pitfalls that End in Losses

As we see on those property television shows, and as my friends Charles and Diana Morgan found out, you can make some pretty bad mistakes that will result in financial losses on your property. If you are not careful and working closely with your Power Pro Team, you could stumble into trouble. Here are some tips to avoid:

1. *Not having a plan.* If you do not have a refurbishment plan before you buy the property, you're not planning well enough. Just letting your contractor go in, ripping everything out and replacing with new can be a waste of money and a waste of your time.

2. *Using emotion when refurbishing.* This is a business and you are in it to generate a passive income for life, so don't use personal touches when plain walls and carpet are fine. Agree a budget and stick with it despite what your inner interior designer tells you!

3. *Not being clear with your refurb team.* Once you have a budget, agree it with the refurb team and get them to sign it so there can be no disagreements at a later date. Pay them in stages as work is finished, and pay the final amount once the snagging list is completed.

4. *Do not overspend but do not cut corners.* You have a responsibility to keep you tenants safe and secure. All fire, gas, and electrical safety checks and equipment must be carried out regularly to fulfil your duty as a landlord. Carrying out all necessary work now will save you having to do it when tenants have already moved in, saving you time and any requests for a reduction in rent.

5. *Do not do unnecessary major works.* Most properties built after the 1960s will not need a complete rewire, for example. If approved to do so by an electrical engineer, installing a new electrical consumer unit, new plug sockets, new light switches and new pendants will give the impression that a complete rewire has been done but for a fraction of the cost.

6. *Underestimating the time needed to refurbish.* Budgeting for two weeks' worth of refurbishment (and hoping for the best) when your property needs four weeks is

going to lose you money. Be realistic when looking at the time needed and get advice from your refurb contractor. Why not offer them a bonus if they can complete the work a week early? Getting a tenant in sooner speeds up your cash-flow.

7. *Doing DIY.* Unless you want another full-time job or have money to burn, it is often quicker to get the experts in to do the work for you. Doing it yourself is a false economy, as Roy Inman found out, and contractors normally get discounts from wholesalers and builders merchants that you won't be able to get.

8. *Keep your refurbishments appropriate.* Do not go crazy spending too much on fancy extras such as wet rooms and luxury kitchens if your target tenants do not need it. The chances are that you will suffer the double whammy of not be able to charge more rent or increase the property value when you come to refinance it. If in doubt, use the 'Spend £1 to Increase the Value by £3 Rule'.

9. *Not finding out about the properties around you.* Find out how you can make your property better by investigating surrounding properties. Ask your letting agent and refurbishment manager for their advice, and if it is within budget, follow it.

10. *Not enhancing any outdoor space.* People like having some space outdoors, so spend some money on your outdoor areas to create 'curb appeal.' Painting the outside of your property and making the space tidy can help it rent out quicker, and can convince the surveyor you have increased the value.

I have shown you how refurbishing properties can generate significant profits, if you do them the right way.

By following these tips and asking your refurbishment team and letting agent for advice, you will be able to master refurbishments like a Property Ironman.

Remember, become good at controlling the costs and you will become great at increasing your profits.

Let us now move to the next step in the Winning 3PR framework. The second 'R' – Rent: Financing Your Lifestyle.

Step 5: Rent - Financing Your Lifestyle

"Ambition fueled by compassion, wisdom, and integrity is a powerful force for good that will turn the wheels of industry and open the doors of opportunity for you and countless others."

ZIG ZIGLAR

Renting out your newly refurbished, clean, and tidy investment property can be traumatic. You have just spent thousands of pounds improving it with the intention of increasing its value, and it is now time to let a complete stranger(s) live in it! In return, you hope they will look after it and pay you some money every month, but there are no guarantees. Is it the right thing to do? Why don't you just sell it? So many things can go wrong!

I will show you throughout this chapter that if you get this step right, you will never worry about your properties again, and they will become your personal cash machines, sending you profitable income every month for as long as you own them. Renting the 3PR way will finance your lifestyle—your only choice is how much money you need!

I wonder if you can relate to this story. Imagine that you have just picked up the keys to a brand new Bugatti Veyron, the fastest street-legal production car in the world. This car is the dream of petrol heads the world over—it is capable of comfortably exceeding 250 miles per hour and costs more than £1 million! This shining black engineering masterpiece is sitting on your driveway outside your house. As soon as you arrive, the front door to your house opens and your teenage son Alexander runs outside to take a look. He has recently passed his driving test and is desperate to sit in the car. You let him climb in, put on the racing harness, and sit back and smell the leather. You know what he's going to ask next, don't you?

"Dad, can I have a quick drive please?"

Your heart sinks for a few seconds, you immediately think about the extortionate figure you had to pay insuring the family to drive it, before you relent and say, *"Go on then son, but you must be back in ten minutes. And don't speed or it will be the last time that you drive it!"*

You watch nervously as he reverses the Bugatti out of the driveway, waves to you, and then carefully drives the car down the street and out of sight. Suddenly you hear the distant roar of the engine as he accelerates out onto the main road.

Those ten minutes seem to be the longest of your life! Your mind starts imagining all sorts of terrible scenarios. You picture a high speed chase with traffic police, other motorists shaking their fists at your speeding son, and children diving out of the way as the super-car races past. You pray that every one of these images does not come true as you anxiously wait for Alexander to come home.

After 14 long and painful minutes, he drives the car down your street and, as he smiles at you apologetically, he parks back in the driveway. As discreetly as you can, your eyes instantly scan the Bugatti's bodywork for any signs of damage, but you are relieved to find no evidence of misadventure. *"Sorry Dad, I didn't realise the time. That was amazing though, thanks!"* From that point on you vow never to let Alexander drive the Bugatti again, it is just too stressful!

This is a similar experience that many novice property investors and first time landlords dread—how do you know your tenants are looking after your property when you are out of sight and out of mind? Anything can happen and you are powerless to stop it!

So let me ask you a question, *'Who thinks it is important to treat your tenants the way you want to be treated yourself?'*

I do too. This is a vital component to building a successful and sustainable property portfolio. Property Ironmen understand that your tenants are the ones who will be paying your mortgage, as well as your passive income, so respect them and treat them well.

Make no mistake, there will always be some bad apples—in among the good tenants and great tenants will be some terrible ones who will cause you some grief. That is just the way it goes, but in my experience, and using the lessons below, you can minimise the impact any bad apples will have. Typically out of 10 or 15 tenants, you might get one who causes you a problem, but even then you will know how to deal with them quickly before replacing them with someone else.

When I started out in property I did not know the first thing about finding tenants or being a professional landlord. I had absolutely no idea how to prepare my property for rent or what rules and regulations I had to be mindful of. Most of the process was a mystery to me.

Old vs. New Rental Possibilities

Becoming a private landlord 20 years ago used to be a very easy option for many because there were so few rules and regulations that they had to abide by. Once investors bought a property they could fill it with any old second-hand furniture, advertise it in the local newspaper, and charge what they wanted in the form of rent. Bad practice and unprofessionalism by many helped create terms such as 'rogue' and 'slum' landlord and they became widely used in the media.

The rules governing the rights of landlords and of tenants have been tightened up considerably in recent years by governments in an attempt to clean up the industry from these bad practices, and to protect both sides when issues arise.

Landlords feared squatters inhabiting their properties if they were empty, for example, and they found it hard and expensive to evict them. The rules on squatters have only recently been amended in the UK to help protect landlords. Tenants, on the other hand, did not have many rights, and could live in unsuitable and unsafe accommodation. If they complained, their options were often either to put up with it or move out (voluntarily or forcibly!)

In today's society, tenants have a right to expect safe and secure housing, and in return landlords have a right to expect to be paid on time and that their property will be looked after.

Private landlords today must ensure they comply by the housing laws, and failure to do so could lead them to be sued by their tenants, fined by the local housing authorities, or even imprisoned.

Rather than scaring you off the prospect of becoming a property investor, it is important that you know the consequences of not being a responsible landlord. Like with all things in the winning 3PR framework, you should leverage the expertise of others in this area so you don't have to learn the legal system yourself.

Your Triathlon Lifestyle

Renting your first property is like taking part in your first Ironman race. It is like nothing you've ever experienced before. The experience itself is terrifying and exhilarating.

My first Ironman took me almost 17 hours to complete, and it was the most painful and rewarding thing I had ever done in my life at that stage. I did not really know what to expect, and I certainly didn't know if I was capable of completing it. Everything was a new experience—the battle to find open water in the melee of a thousand other swimmers, the realisation that my legs would have to power my bike up yet another Alpine mountain, and the mental doubts that creep in during the marathon when your body is almost completely exhausted.

But like in an Ironman race, careful preparation before you start to look for tenants can stop many of those doubts and help ensure that managing your property is pain-free.

So let's start to look at what you need to do with your property to make it easy to rent out.

How do you prepare your property for rent?

- *Neutral interiors.* Whether you are renting to students, a family, or a professional working couple, one rule applies to the interiors—keep it neutral! That means white or magnolia walls and brown or grey plain carpets. A good paint finish makes any property look clean and spacious.

- *Provide basic appliances to attract good tenants.* It is a good idea to buy white goods to attract the best tenants. Appliances such as dishwashers and washing machines are often expected by tenants. They are relatively inexpensive to buy and have up to five year guarantees, again a 'must have' if you want to take away some of the potential landlord stresses—repairs and floods.

- *Get a professional to do the refurbishments.* You can spot amateur DIY fixes a mile away. Never, ever do a cheap job. It will cause higher maintenance and repair costs later. A useful guide for any newbie property landlord is that tenants will not put up with broken appliances or poor decor for long, it is their home after all.

- *Create a 'snag' list of any issues in the property that haven't been fixed before renting it.* The minor finishing details that often get missed after a refurb, such as paint splashes on tiles or doors that don't close property, can be annoying for tenants. Do not give them a reason to choose another property over yours. Getting these jobs finished is not expensive, and they do make a difference.

- *Comply with all safety requirements.* I know this was covered in the refurbishment chapter in Step 4, but it is so important that I wanted to highlight it again! Protecting your tenants is as important as protecting your property. There you go—I promise I will not mention it any more.

- *Furnish student and professional house share property.* Providing inexpensive but good quality furniture and kitchenware helps to 'sell' your property to these types of tenant. There are a range of good furniture manufacturers around, such as Ikea, that enable you to fully furnish the property for not a lot of money. Similarly, you will be surprised at how the use of little modern touches such as contemporary prints from artists such as Banksy can help get the tenants through your door.

- *Provide an information pack about your property.* This is a simple document that informs your tenants about the local area, how to work everything in the property, what they can expect from you as the landlord, and what you expect from them. Transport links, local grocery stores, local amenities, when the rubbish is collected, and emergency contact numbers are all helpful. Instructions on how to work the heating, boiler, and other appliances will stop late night or weekend calls from tenants. Stating how you expect them to behave and what they can expect from you also makes it clear from the beginning of any tenancy what the house rules are. I find these information packs help prevent many potential issues resulting in less hassle for you (or your letting agent - more on that in a minute!).

Now that we have covered some tips that will help your property rent out quickly, how do you find the best tenants to start paying for your lifestyle?

First things first, never manage your own properties! The whole aim of the Winning 3PR framework is to give you passive income—that means leverage the expertise of others. I strongly advise anyone against managing their own properties. Admittedly it is not an onerous task if you have invested in one local property, but if your area is miles away from where you live or you have multiple properties, it is just not worth it. If you think it will save you money, it is a false economy (remember the story of my friend Robert?)

Find a good letting agent and get them on your Power Pro Team. They will save you any unnecessary 'voids' (periods of time when your property is not rented out, but you still have bills to pay) by finding you good tenants, quickly replacing any bad apples, and stopping you from getting the panicked tenant phone calls or emails at all times of day and night because they don't know how to replace a light bulb!

If you still want to manage your properties despite my warning, that is your choice, but I think you are mad! Whatever direction you take, I have provided some pointers below that you or your letting agent should follow to find the best tenants.

- *Find an excellent letting agent.* You need a proactive agent with a good track record, who will work hard on your behalf, recommendations are best. Ideally, they will already rent out similar properties to your own, know the tenant demand, and be a property investor themselves. If they invest in the area too, they will understand exactly how to help you achieve the best returns and minimise voids. Quick tip: make sure they know what 'yield' is - don't laugh, you'd be surprised at how many have not got a clue!

- *Set a reasonable rental price.* Always set the rent at a figure that is in keeping in the local area. Some landlords hold out for the highest price they can get in the hope to make the highest profit possible, but by asking for £100 a month more than anyone else and having your property empty for a month or more does not make business sense. If you are concerned about voids, why not reduce your rent by 5% to fill it quickly, and you can always increase it again in the next tenancy period.

- *Advertise your property.* The chances are that the more people know your property is available, the quicker you will rent it out. Postcards in local shops and adverts in local newspapers do work, but online marketing is a very effective promotional tool that must be used. Online advertising can also be tracked, which is something that more traditional advertising methods cannot offer. Websites such as Gumtree, Spareroom, and Easyroommate are all great sites to advertise your property to tenants who are actively looking for a home. Listing your property on portals such as Rightmove and Zoopla are also effective.

- *Do refurbishment viewings.* A tip that I have used to minimise the time between the refurbishment being completed and renting out a house is to hold viewings while the work is still going on. I only do this when all the major work has been finished and the final decorating, minor snagging work or carpeting needs to be done. Many prospective tenants like this because they can see that they will be getting a 'brand new' home, and a few times I have moved the refurb team out the day before the tenants move in.

- *Always check out your tenants.* You or your letting agent must do adequate checks on your potential tenants. It is advisable to check their identification, current and previous landlord references, current and previous employers' references. If you are renting out to students, get a guarantor (often a parent or guardian), and if you are renting out to anyone on benefits check with the local council benefits office. It is easy to do these checks yourself, but if you want a third-party to do it for you there are companies such as www.upad. co.uk who can do it cheaply and quickly. These checks might sound onerous, but they can flag up potential issues and isn't it better to know who will be living in your house before they move in? A good track record means that you are less likely to have worry about your payments coming in each month.

- *Meet your prospective tenants.* I like to meet my tenants, so often do the viewings myself. I know my property better than anyone else, so I can tell them all the benefits of it, explain what is around the local area, and give any tips on the best places to shop, have coffee, or grab a bite to eat. It also means that I know the tenant has the correct basic information about the rent, tenancy period, and inclusion of bills before they move in—it just helps set expectations on all sides.

- *Demonstrate how everything works when they move in.* This is a really easy thing to do, but many don't bother, and it can stop those panicked phone calls. Physically showing how the heating works and how to turn the mains water off in case of a leak, for example, really helps you and the tenant.

- *Fix any problems quickly.* Once a tenant has moved in to your property and they complain about something that is broken or needs repairing, do it quickly. Failing to maintain the property can lead to higher tenant 'churn' - they will just look for a better house elsewhere. This can increase your costs to find new tenants as well as make it more likely that you will have voids.

- *Deal with any problem tenants quickly.* You need to know the landlord rules and regulations that need to be followed if you have to get rid of a bad apple. It is advisable that you know the basics, but unless you want to learn the legal requirements and processes that must be followed yourself, I would advise you once again to use a letting agent to manage that for you.

These simple tips can help you find the best tenants. Working in partnership with your letting agent to maintain your property, and looking after your tenants, is the most effective way I know of ensuring a stress-free property portfolio.

The Property Ironman wants passive income to achieve the triathlon lifestyle, and the thrill you get of seeing the first monthly rental payment hit your bank account shows you are on your way to financial freedom.

Learning how to rent your property correctly will help you build multiple income streams that will provide for you and your family for the rest of your life.

Proof That Renting Results in Profit

You have already read about some of the everyday people I know who are successful property investors and now make a great monthly income from renting their properties out. First there was Julie Hogbin who makes £700 per month and only started investing at the beginning of 2012; Simon Zutshi told us he receives more than £7,000 per month and aims to get £10,000 before long; then there was Roy Inman who already makes £10,000; and finally Gill Alton who makes more than £7,000 every month from rental income. I'm sure you agree that these figures are incredible and probably enough for most people reading this book to live comfortably.

Well, I am now going to tell you about another case study from a really unique couple who are making a big impression in the UK property investing field.

Case Study: *Francis and Emily Dolley*

Francis and Emily are a father and daughter team who, together with Mum Jane and son James, have created a family portfolio worth more than £1.8m, and their property income is £10,000 every month—much of it from properties they don't even own themselves! This was all created in the last three years.

Francis was a disgruntled builder who wanted a change in his life, and ironically it took him a long time to decide that property was the best way he could make his wealth and provide for his family. Emily graduated with an architecture and planning degree, and on leaving university the only job she found was in a local telephone call centre, which she hated. After six months she joined the rest of the family in the property business and hasn't looked back since.

The Dolleys are the UK property equivalent of the Von Trapps (I must ask Francis if they sing too!). Every one of them has a defined role in the family property business, and if you haven't heard of them yet, you will do soon.

Based in South West England, they initially bought some two and three bed single let properties before buying a six bed house of multiple occupation (HMO). After that they turned their attention to what they now call their 'Multi-Let Cashflow System', which involves turning old student accommodation in Bristol into desirable homes for young professionals.

Managing tenants is one of the most important aspects of property according to Francis, and that means treating them well and dealing with any problems quickly.

"This is a people industry and not giving your tenants a reason to withhold rent is imperative. I had a tenant complain about damp a few months ago. She called in the morning and I supplied a nice new and very quiet dehumidifier within a few hours. We sorted the problem the next day and left her a bottle of wine for her trouble."

The effort that Francis and Emily put in to keep their tenants happy means that most of their tenants will stay with them for a very long time. This keeps the rental profits rolling in every month.

Due to their persistence, the Dolley family are happier and wealthier and enjoying life more than ever.

If you would like to hear more from this very entertaining family and get some great insights into how they have become successful, please go to my website: **www.thepropertyironman.com**

10 Rental Disasters That Lose You Money

There are times when even the most cautious Property Ironmen can be caught out, and leave themselves vulnerable to financial losses. Here are 10 rental disasters that you need to avoid:

1. *Let out properties yourself.* Do not create a full-time job for yourself; let a professional letting agent do it for you. A great agent will work hard for their monthly fee and save you time, worry, effort, and money.

2. *Don't adequately check out your tenants.* Doing partial checks or none at all means you might get a bad apple who damages your property, fails to pay your rent, or disrupts other tenants or neighbours. It is not worth the risk.

3. *Don't advertise your property online.* There are so many easy ways to get your property advert in front of prospective tenants, so make use of them. The quicker you rent it out, the sooner the profits come in. Here's another tip: even if your property is fully tenanted, keep the contact details of everyone responding to your ad as you might have something for them in the future. You have paid to find these tenants once, so start a database so you don't have to pay to find them again.

4. *Not doing an inventory check.* Failing to adequately fill out an inventory check with your tenant as they move in, and getting them to sign it, can leave you open to a dispute if anything is lost or damaged when it is time for them to move out. Protect yourself by videoing the inventory check with a date stamp. No one can argue with that!

5. *Not complying with all landlord rules and regulations.* I know I promised not to mention it again, but I lied! It's important. But I think you realise that now. If in doubt, get advice from a letting agent or a solicitor. Enough said.

6. *Not repairing damage quickly.* Tenants resent it if reasonable repairs are not made quickly, especially if it involves the water, heating, or electrics in the property. They could request a refund from the rent, take less care of your property, or worse. Follow Francis's example!

7. *Hold out for the highest possible rent.* If your property is empty for more than a month because you are asking for an extortionately high rent, you are losing money. Take a longer term view, fill your property quickly, and increase the rent slightly after the first tenancy period comes to an end.

8. *Not adequately insuring your property.* Insure your property when you exchange contracts. Adequate insurance will protect you from damage or theft during the refurbishment and then through the tenancy term. Insuring against void periods can also give you the ultimate peace of mind that many property investors want.

9. *Not putting the tenant deposit in a protected scheme.* This is not your money. If nothing is broken or missing at the end of the tenancy, the deposit must by law be returned to them.

10. *Not saving any of the profit to cover repairs.* I recommend five percent of the rental income to cover minor repairs. You will need to spend this money at some stage on your property, so allocate it from the start. Getting into this habit will cover you for most unexpected bills.

This chapter discussed Step 5 in my winning 3PR framework, Rent - Financing your Lifestyle. It showed how Property Ironmen follow some simple do's and don't's to effectively manage their properties so that they start generating monthly profit.

The key learning is this: Look After Your Tenants & Your Tenants Will Look After You.

Now it is time to move on to the last part of the winning 3PR framework, Refinance - Recycle Your Cash. This step shows you how to release some or all of your initial investment so you can grow your portfolio until you are financially free.

Step 6: Refinance - Recycle Your Cash

"I made a tremendous amount of money on real estate. I'll take real estate rather than go to Wall Street and get 2.8 percent. Forget about it."

IVANA TRUMP

We have now come to Step 6 in the winning 3PR framework, which is all about Refinance - Recycle Your Cash. If you learn how to get this step right, you can recycle most or all of your initial investment funds to buy more property. Although there isn't a huge amount to learn in this step, it is easy to get it wrong—and that could mean the property portfolio you want to build grinds to a halt before it really gets started.

This part of the framework is the one step that can make your quest for a growing and sustainable passive income a reality. So who wants to learn some great tips that will help you get your cash out of your property quickly so you can keep buying? In that case, read on!

This final step requires a mortgage surveyor to revalue your newly refurbished property at a higher amount, so you can borrow against that figure and release the funds to buy again.

This reminds me of an incident that happened more than 15 years ago that made such an impact on me that I've never forgotten it.

When I was 24 years old, I had my first 'proper' job in advertising, and I was part of the financial client sales team on the national newspaper. I worked with a great man who became a close friend of mine called Nicholas Hill. Despite being Irish by birth, he had a very deep voice and spoke with a perfect English accent. As he was so well-spoken, his work colleagues nicknamed him 'Dear Boy'—a phrase he called every man in the department, in fact every man he ever met! As I was a relatively inexperienced member of the team, Nick took me under his wing and showed me how things were done. I learnt my job the Nicholas Hill way.

Nick was a true gentlemen and a real bon viveur. He was a tall and imposing man, with a shock of white hair, quick to smile and always dressed in a pinstripe suit and colourful tie.

Nick was also a great raconter and seemed to have an endless supply of hilarious stories for every occasion. He lived life to the full and was always the life and soul of any party.

One Thursday in May he invited me to a client lunch at a restaurant I had never heard of before. It was Simpsons in the Strand, in London, and for those who do not know, it is a very traditional and established restaurant that has fed many famous and influential people over the last 170 years.

We arrived outside Simpsons by taxi, got out, and entered the main entrance door and walked into the dining room. It was an incredible sight! The room was enormous, it had a double or triple height ceiling, a dozen great chandeliers that lit up the room, and a huge display of flowers by the grand piano in the corner, where soft music was being played. The walls were covered in ancient wood panels, the ceiling was ornately carved, and the tables had thick white tablecloths, linen napkins, silver cutlery, and heavy crystal glasses. I was only 24 and had never been to a place like this before, it just blew me away. I also felt very self-conscious and was terrified of doing something wrong in front of the Maitre'd!

This being a traditional English restaurant that was proud of its heritage, the client, Nick, and I all ordered their famous roast lunch with all the trimmings. Nick also ordered a fine bottle of Bordeaux to go with our meal—this was how things were done in the advertising world of the 1990s (at least it was according to the rules of Mr. N. Hill!). He leaned over to me and said quietly, *"Jamie, dear boy, enjoy yourself. You will love it here!"*

As well as the incredible decor, what struck me was how friendly everyone was, and how they all seemed to know

Nick. It turned out he had been coming to Simpsons for more than 20 years and was a very regular customer.

When our lunch was ready, several waiters came to our table and laid down three large silver cloches in front of us. These were silver domes that covered the plates, and I assumed they were to keep the food warm. Without speaking a word, they all lifted the cloches off in unison to reveal the feast underneath. It was a really theatrical display, aimed to show off the food in the most impressive way possible as well as bring a sense of occasion to our lunch. It certainly did the trick, and whenever I think of Nick today I remember that lunch very fondly!

This is very similar to what you are trying to do as a Property Ironman in Step 6 when the surveyor comes to do your property revaluation. You need to put on a display so that your property looks impressive and the surveyor is left in no doubt that the value of it has been enhanced.

Old vs. New Investments

Property Ironmen understand that the only manageable and sustainable way to achieve true financial freedom is to invest in assets that generate passive income. This enables your time and energy to be spent on the more important things in life (unless you want to keep on working in a job of course!).

In the old days, it was easier to refinance your properties because the market was rising and lending companies were literally falling over themselves to give you more money to buy more property. It didn't matter if you were not credit worthy and didn't have an income; you could use a 'self-certification' mortgage, which meant you did not have to prove you could afford the loan (some called these products 'liar loans'!)

Similarly, many investors used to be able to invest in no money down (NMD) deals where they used bridging finance to avoid paying the deposit from their own funds. The investor needed two willing solicitors to obscure the fact that the bridging loan was the source of the buy-to-let mortgage. The buyer would agree to buy a property at a large discount, telling the first solicitor that they wanted to borrow against the full market value, not the discounted price, from a mortgage lender. The buyer gets bridging finance and pays the first solicitor the minimum deposit for the purchase. On completion, the second solicitor returns the difference between the discount and the real market price from the seller to the buyer, who then pays off the bridging loan.

This is now mortgage fraud, and the Council of Mortgage Lenders have tightened up their lending criteria so that self-certification mortgages and NMD deals are now illegal. The regulators also now insist that property buyers must own property for a minimum of six months before they can refinance it—they have done this to stop investors refinancing on the same day as the original purchase or soon afterwards.

Another regular practice by property investors over the last ten years or so was to keep refinancing the value of their portfolios up to the maximum amount possible. This enabled them to squeeze every last penny out of their properties, while reducing their equity, so they could build up very large portfolios, very quickly. In the rising market, many assumed that property prices would continue to go up indefinitely. However, when the market turned, lenders started reassessing the value of investor's portfolios and increased borrowing rates or called in their loans. The result for many investors was that they went bankrupt because they did not adequately plan their finances and they got caught out by their greed.

It is important that you understand how the property market has changed and how the regulations have been adapted since the last property bubble. As I stated at the beginning of this book, property investing is not a 'get rich quick' scheme but you can still work within the rules and generate significant wealth over time. It just takes realism and persistence.

My winning 3PR framework works in today's market and is relevant now. These old practices no longer work, and now you know why.

So let's now focus on what you need to do to get the right value for your refinanced property.

Your Recycled Returns

Refinancing your property the Property Ironman way is all about recycling your cash so you can invest again in a safe and responsible way. In this step, the mortgage broker on your Power Pro Team really proves his or her worth. He or she already understands your investing strategy, knows your financial status, and now needs to find you the most appropriate refinancing solution, out of all the mortgage products on the market. That solution should enable you to recycle some or all of your money.

Depending on your circumstances, they might advise you to look at commercial lending over standard buy-to-let mortgage products. Commercial lending is a useful source of finance, but you need to consider some of the potential pros and cons of using it over standard retail lending.

Here are some of the benefits that commercial lending can give you:

- Often the rent needs to cover 160% or more of the monthly mortgage payment, but this can come down to 70% over time (which is comparable to standard buy-to-let products).

- You can choose your own surveyor, which can give you an element of certainty if you have found one who has given you favourable revaluations in the past.

- Some value your property based on the income it yields, not on the comparable price of others in the same street. If the typical 'bricks and mortar' valuation for a property is £80,000 from a retail lender, for example, a commercial lender might calculate its value to be £110,000 because they have taken into account the annual rental income that the property generates. In this example the extra £30,000 in lending can finance another property purchase.

- There is often no limit to how much you can borrow, so you might start off with more than £1m.

- Some lenders are flexible on the type of properties they will lend on, such as fire-damaged property, which is something most retail buy-to-let lenders would shy away from.

Some of the negatives about commercial lending are that they will be repayment mortgages, the rates are often higher than standard buy-to-let mortgages, and they can be more difficult to arrange as you need to provide detailed financial plans (profit and loss account, a balance sheet, rental forecasts etc.)

The key difference, though, is that commercial lending is based on having a personal commercial relationship with the lender, and decisions are usually based on detailed conversations about your business, between you and the commercial account manager.

This means that over time, as the relationship and understanding of your business strengthens, the lending criteria can become more flexible. In contrast, standard retail buy-to-let lending decisions are often computerised decisions based on your relative 'tick box' score against their lending criteria. Please note that commercial lending is not suitable or available to everyone, and this is where your mortgage broker can advise you.

Assuming that you opt for a standard buy-to-let mortgage product when refinancing, it is vital that you create a dossier of evidence for the surveyor that supports how much you think it is now worth. The essential elements include the following:

- 'Before' and 'after' photographs of the property before you did the work and once it was completed. The stark contrast is a visual reminder that you have worked hard on improving the property, and as it has been rented out for at least six months, it proves you have created an investment that generates monthly income.

- A list of works that were carried out with a breakdown of the costs too. Receipts are useful as well so you can prove how much was spent on renovations. Sometimes a cursory glance might suggest that all you have done is lay new carpets and given the place a lick of paint, when actually you might have rewired the house, installed central heating and a new bathroom!

- Lastly you need some independent evidence that shows recent sold prices for similar properties in the local area. If you are asking for a revaluation of £100,000, for example, having three properties selling for or above that price in the last three months makes your argument stronger. These can be found on property portals such as Rightmove and on the Land Registry website. You might also consider getting a 'realtime' valuation from a company such as Hometrack.co.uk. This online valuation service is used by many lenders, and for a small fee it can also support your evidence.

Getting your dossier ready before the surveyor visits your property is an essential tool for any Property Ironman, and it gives you confidence.

When the surveyor does inspect your property, meet them and show them around. Giving them your dossier and discussing your property demonstrates professionalism and will help build rapport with them. You never know if this surveyor will be one of the 'friendly' ones who you will want to use again on your next property, so treat them well and be as helpful as you can.

These simple but effective tips can really make the difference to the money you can release from your properties. They are the exact same strategies that I use with all my revaluations, and although there are no guarantees, they certainly help.

That said, putting a valuation on anything is subjective and sometimes surveyors will not raise the value as much as you might want. This could be for a number of reasons and occasionally lenders direct their surveyors to be more conservative in the valuations if they are concerned about market conditions.

If this happens to you, ask your mortgage broker to appeal the revaluation and refer back to your dossier. Providing the evidence and escalating the problem up the chain of command at the lending company can work in your favour at times.

The upside results in the lender refinancing your property and releasing funds back to you so you can buy again. Depending on the new mortgage you have secured, the equity in your property will still be between 20% - 25%, it is just against the new, higher value. It is up to you to either keep the amount of lending at the same level or to leave some of the cash in the property and start paying down more of the debt.

If you do not get the revaluation price that was expected, then the downside is normally minimal. You can wait for a longer period of time before refinancing again (do not forget to update your dossier), and in the meantime the rental returns on your money left in to the property will still be much higher than you can earn in any savings account- so you are still making a great return! Here are some examples to demonstrate what I mean.

Examples of Refinanced Properties for Profit

I have included a selection of properties purchased in 2012 that have gone through the full 'purchase, refurbish, rent and refinance' cycle to give you proof that this strategy works.

Example 1: A three bed house was bought for £68,000 (24% below market value) and £7,000 was spent on the refurbishment. It was later revalued at £90,000 and £17,000 was returned after refinancing, leaving £6,000 of the original investment in the house. Although I didn't get all my initial funds back out of the property on revaluation, the funds left in deliver an annual return of 64% (i.e. annual rental profit, divided by money left in the house). I'm not unhappy with that, and with the remainder of the released cash I put it towards another property purchase.

Example 2: A two bed house was bought for £63,000 (26 % Below Market Value) and £2,500 was spent on the refurbishment. After being revalued at £85,000 over £16,500 was returned after refinancing, leaving £2,750 of the original funds in the property. I got most of my initial investment returned to me (deposit, refurbishment costs, legal and broker fees) and the money left in the house delivers a 114% return on investment (i.e. annual rental profit, divided by the money left in the house).

Example 3: A two bed house was bought for £50,000 (33% below market value) and it required a minor refurbishment which cost just over £2,000. It was later revalued at £75,000 meaning that almost £19,000 was returned after refinancing and none of the original funds were left in the property. This house generates an 11% rental yield making it a great cash flowing property too! You can guess what happened to the £19,000 can't you? Yes, you're right, it went towards the next property purchase!

Refinancing Case Study: Neil Larken

The above examples are far from unique, and I want to share with you another great case study from an investor friend of mine who has created a monthly profitable cash-flow of more than £8,000 in just three years. Wouldn't you want to do that too?!

Neil Larken was a hardworking, self-employed civil engineer who got paid by the hour and often worked seven days a week just to make ends meet. He was fed up with his job and knew he had to change direction in his life. In June 2009, Neil and his business partner Chris Smith both started investing around Blackpool in the North West of England. Today the portfolio is worth £3.675m, and they have over £1.25m in equity. How does that sound after only three years?

Neil attributes a large element of their success down to the business relationships and lending facilities that they have secured with commercial banks. Buying properties and refinancing them as soon as the refurbishments have finished (often in only a few months) has meant that they have been able to get most of their funds returned quickly so they can buy again.

"We've had so much trouble with normal buy-to-let lenders. We stay away from them - it just doesn't work for us", says Neil.

Neil also said his mortgage broker was the only reason why they could get in front of the commercial lenders in the first place. A personal recommendation from him meant they soon started working with Aldermore, Lloyds TSB, and the Co-operative. They would have struggled to achieve this if they were trying this alone—again reinforcing the benefit of having a strong Power Pro Team around you. Property is a people business where recommendations and referrals can literally open the doors to huge opportunities.

Neil believes in taking massive action and in his case the results speak for themselves!

If you would like to hear the rest of my very candid interview with Neil, you can access it at: **www.thepropertyironman.com**

10 Refinance Mistakes That Cost You Money

There are many ways that you can get refinancing wrong, resulting in a low valuation for your property. Here are the most common mistakes that novice investors make and the simple actions you can take so that you don't fall into the same trap.

- *Failing to take 'before and after' photos of your refurbishment.* This evidence will often help your case with the surveyor

- *Not keeping all refurbishment receipts.* Proving what you have spent can swing revaluations in your favour.

- *Not having comparable sold prices.* Have a record of at least three comparable properties to yours that have sold in the last three months.

- *Using the same surveyor to value your property after six months.* Using the same one will not result in an increase in value, despite your refurbishment efforts, so go for a different surveyor.

- *Not knowing which surveyors lenders use.* Many nationwide surveying companies are affiliated with specific lenders, so just chose a different mortgage lender for the refinancing of your property. They will not know what you paid for your property and will make a valuation based on their own findings and the evidence you provide.

- *Having a poor mortgage broker.* You need one that covers the whole of market, and who really understands your strategy, so he or she can advise you of the most suitable products that are available.

- *Failing to challenge a low valuation.* If the surveyor comes back with a valuation for your property that you think is low, you must always challenge it. Having a good mortgage broker on your Power Pro Team means he or she can do that for you.

- *Not being at the property when it is being valued.* It is important to meet the surveyor so you can hand over your evidence and talk about what you have done to improve the property.

- *Not using an independent surveyor to challenge the lenders valuation.* Although this will cost you a small amount, an independent RICS valuation on your property might help your case when challenging a lower than expected valuation. If it succeeds, the extra funds that are returned to you will make the extra cost money well spent.

- *Not considering commercial finance.* Commercial lending can be more flexible over the longer term and it can open up another source of funding. Here's a tip for you: if you pay all your rental income into your commercial bank account, they will see that the regular income and it will help your relationship with the lender.

You now know what to do, and what not to do, to master the art of refinancing. Using these techniques in a responsible way is the key to building a sustainable property portfolio for you and your family.

Please remember this: **Present your property well and profit will be your Present.**

That's it folks, we have completed my *proven* winning 3PR framework. This last step is the culmination of all that has gone on before. Having chosen where to buy and what to invest in and used your pro team to purchase the property at the best price, you have completed a cost-effective refurbishment, and rented it out to generate a profitable monthly income. In addition to that, you have successfully revalued the property so that some or all of your initial investment has been returned to you after refinancing. With the money back in your pocket, you can go again.

Triathlons are exactly the same. All those months of

training and preparation, careful course selection, investing in the right kit, and support from your pro team, means you power through on race day to complete the Ironman in a personal best time. You cross the finish line, hang the medal around your neck, and look back on all that you have achieved. You are now ready to do it all over again and complete in another race!

By implementing the six steps in my winning 3PR framework, you now have the tools necessary to become a *Property Ironman*.

Auto Pilot: Keep on Winning

"Winning is not a sometime thing; it's an all the time thing. You don't win once in a while, you don't do things right once in a while, you do them right all the time. Winning is habit. Unfortunately, so is losing."

VINCE LOMBARDI

If you want to keep on winning, then you're going to have to create systems and procedures to take much of the guess work out of your business so that it can run on autopilot.

Now, autopilot doesn't mean you abandon the race and let it run on its own. As an Ironman, if you're not taking part in the race you can't win it! Autopilot simply means that your property investment business is streamlined so that it runs like a well-oiled machine.

Building Your Property Empire

A property empire for you can be anything from five to more than 100 properties. Sir Alan Sugar, for example, has thousands of properties, retail centres, and prestigious commercial buildings. If you're going to build your property empire, autopilot will help you manage it—whatever the size. Here's how you do it:

- *Make sure that your criteria for buying property is set in stone and will always guarantee your success.* Yes, you can be slightly flexible if you need to—but this is more like a rule than a guideline. It exists to keep you thinking about the profit that you have to make.

- *Create processes for everything.* What is the best way to find properties? What scripts are used when speaking to new estate agents? What highly effective procedures can you implement to keep your refurbishments running as smoothly and efficiently as possible? Write everything down.

- *Adhere to financial constraints.* If you do not buy property that fits in with your financial model, then you're going to get yourself into trouble, and you may even lose money. If you set your discount rate at 25%

and the target rental yield at 10%, then don't buy below that. It is that simple!

- *Create policies for your team.* You Power Pro Team assist you every day, so write down what you expect of them and what they can expect from you. Create policies for them and get them involved in making them with you —this helps get their buy in and ensures that nothing is missed. Let them know what they can and can't do. For most scenarios, you need your team to know immediately how you expect them to react.

- *Set a structure for yourself.* In the beginning, you will be more hands-on than you will be after a few years down the line. You are working for yourself now, and you will need daily routines. For example, I plan on completing three daily tasks that will move my property business forward. I get up early and complete the task that I perceive to be the hardest, to get it out of the way, and then work on the other two. Once those tasks have been completed the rest of the day is my own.

If you are going to build a property empire, you can't leave the way your business runs to chance. Establishing rules or guidelines to work with might appear to be a waste of time initially, but believe me, it is worth it as it will save you a lot of wasted time, effort, and worry if you know that the business is being run the way you want it.

Love them or hate them, fast-food restaurant, such as McDonald's, only work as efficiently and as profitably as they do because they systemise every part of the burger-making process. Anyone who joins their company learns the processes and these help eliminate uncertainty and guesswork. The result is that a McDonald's burger is the same in Moscow, Madrid, Miami, or Manchester.

The People Business

When you work as a Property Ironman, you might be surprised to find how people-orientated property can be. You need to be able to work well with people. As we humans all think for ourselves, we can be an unpredictable bunch, which makes automation harder, but it is therefore imperative that you get your team to work as efficiently as possible.

I found one key element is required in order for my team to be as efficient and automated as they are—and that's communication. I encourage a consistent stream of communication or feedback between everyone, all day, every day if need be.

Using my winning 3PR framework, buying property is largely sequential, and often one team member is waiting on some information from another team member before they progress with what they need to do.

Technology helps massively in today's world, and it keeps everyone in the team informed on what's happening. All documents, property photos, and refurbishment videos are digitally scanned and saved into Evernote and accessible by the whole team from any Smartphone or computer. Project management software such as Basecamp is great at keeping the team informed as to where any new property is within the 3PR framework. Weekly Skype video calls allow everyone to talk as a group, and any action, problems, or issues are addressed quickly.

None of the members of my Power Pro Team are my employees. They have their own jobs, families, and lives outside of my property portfolio, and I respect that. That's why modern technology is used in an attempt to automate how we work—it saves their time and my time.

We are not perfect and do not always get it right, but we are trying to worker smarter. A successful Property Ironman does not want to work *in their business*, they want to work *on their business*.

The 'Secret' Financial Freedom Formula

My 'secret' financial freedom formula isn't much of a secret to you anymore! I use my winning 3PR framework to earn passive income from my rental properties.

Financial management is vital if you want to automate your property business. All payments in and all payments out of my bank account are on direct debit or standing order. You must ensure that no payments are missed, especially on any loans such as mortgages, because you will be charged fees and it will put a negative mark against your credit score. You need to protect and nurture your credit score like it's your youngest child because otherwise it could stop you borrowing in future. I subscribe to credit reference agencies (such as Equifax and Experien) to keep an eye on my credit score and to help protect me against identity fraud.

I know this is common sense, but it is also worth checking your bank statements monthly for any unexpected transactions. On quite a few occasions my bank has mistakenly taken out multiple payments for the same product or service, and you need to get your cash back quickly. As your property portfolio grows the number of transactions through your bank account seem to multiply exponentially, and you need the eyes of a hawk to spot any inconsistencies!

So, the not-so-secret 'secret' financial formula is this: invest in assets that give you passive income, keep an eye on your bank account, pay all loans on time, protect your credit score, and save as much of your passive income as you can.

This will be much, much simpler when you've grown your property portfolio substantially.

Managing your passive income will determine how far you get in the property game. If you are able to live comfortably and save money, you can expand your property empire quicker than the average property investor.

Remember that the entire point of your passive income stream is to set you financially free.

Knowledge, Learning, and Training for Your Next Race

Completing your first Ironman race or buying your first investment property gives you a similar experience—you feel incredible pride, you are satisfied that all the work has paid off, and most of all you want to shout out "I have done it!" Suddenly, those self-doubts and the worries that weighed heavily on your shoulders disappear, and you get a new found feeling of confidence.

The minute you finish your Ironman race and the thrill and adrenaline has worn off, you're back to thinking how you could have done it better. That's human nature. Ironman competitions are a very good challenge and reward system, which I suppose is why I'm so drawn to them.

Every time I compete I get a little more knowledge, a little more experience, and a little more hunger to push myself physically. When I enter the next big event, I will map out a training program that (hopefully) will make me faster too.

One day I realized that I was not doing this as a property investor. I mean I was going through the motions and growing my portfolio—but was I really trying to improve my personal best? A lot of us need to ask ourselves that question too!

In property investment, the next race is your next property purchase. It's why you learn, and grow, and want to be a better investor. Making small improvements in the systems you use to find, purchase, refurbish, rent, and refinance your properties are always needed to make you better. This is an iterative process, and the results might be that you get better at negotiating bigger discounts, better at controlling refurbishment costs, or faster at getting good tenants. Small 'tweaks' can all add up to make a big improvement in monthly cash flow.

Putting your property investment business on autopilot is a great way to make a lot of money over time, but do not use the fact that passive income is coming into your bank account as an excuse to get lazy.

Successful property investing is incredibly rewarding and very thrilling, just like my Ironman experiences. That is why my advice to you would be to put yourself on autopilot to constantly outdo yourself and become a better, more efficient investor.

Your next race is always on the way in my winning 3PR framework. If you can improve each time and show the world how good you are—it is not going to be long until you are financially free and on your way to considerable wealth and happiness.

Your Success Hurdles

"I've come to believe that each of us has a personal calling that's as unique as a fingerprint - and that the best way to succeed is to discover what you love and then find a way to offer it to others in the form of service, working hard, and also allowing the energy of the universe to lead you."

OPRAH WINFREY

The most difficult thing to do in property investment is not assembling your team or learning how property finance works. It's not calculating the right rental yields or making sure that your properties comply with the required safety regulations.

The most difficult thing to do is—to START. My winning 3PR framework is simple to follow, and many people who are interested in property investing already know some of the basics. But why will most people never do anything about it? The answer is that they are too afraid. There are many success hurdles in life that you need to get over before you can become a Property Ironman, and I'm going to run through some of the most common ones now.

Getting Your Strong Finish

Once you have learned how the 3PR framework works and have started to implement it, you just need to keep doing it, again and again. The simplicity of the framework is its strength, but this can also make students question how powerful it can be for them. However, not understanding what you are trying to get out of it often leads novice investors to give up too soon because they are not tracking how far they have come.

Think about what your strong finish will be. Where do you want to get to? In my first Ironman, I just wanted to be able to finish the race, so that was my goal. In property investing you should decide how much money you need every month to be comfortable or financially free. Some might need £3,000 per month, some might want £5,000 per month, and others might need £10,000 or more per month.

Having your end goal in mind helps you push towards it. I can't explain the thrill of tracking yourself and getting closer, month by month, to your target.

Knowing that in a short amount of time you could be financially stable, and then soon after that financially free, is a very powerful motivator. No money worries, no stress, only working if you want to, and spending more time with your loved ones. That's the ideal isn't it?

So, do that now—make a commitment and write down how much you need.

Then get in contact with me at Jamie@thepropertyironman. com when you've done it, and let me know how you are getting on—it is great to hear when students are beginning to see the results they want!

Knocking Down Financial Hurdles

In sport, a hurdle is something that blocks your path that you have to leap over at great speed in order to win the race. There are many financial hurdles that are difficult to overcome in the average person's life.

Are you one of those people whose first thought is, *"I can't afford to invest in property…?"* The number one excuse I hear from people is that they can't afford it. If you truly understand the financial benefits that you and your loved ones can achieve by following my winning 3PR framework, you would not use lack of money as an excuse to avoid getting started.

I know life can be tough, especially if you are working all the hours that you can just to get by. Some people are lucky enough to have a pot of money to help them get started, but most do not. My friend Neil Larkin, who you read about earlier, refinanced his home to release some funds and did not pay himself for two years while his investments got off the ground. I did the same—I released some equity from my home to buy my first investment properties. *Can you do this too?*

If this is not an option for you, can you borrow funds from friends or family and create a joint venture agreement to share the properties you buy? Deena Honey is an incredible lady from the UK who educated herself in property and within six months had managed to raise more than £500,000 in joint venture finance. Depending on where you live, you won't need much to start. Get talking to friends and family and if they are interested to work with you, get legal advice on how to set up a simple joint venture agreement.

I use a legal document called a deed of trust with my JV partners so that all equity and rental income is shared between us. I use my expertise to find, refurbish, and rent out the property we buy together, and my partners put in the initial funds. There is no reason why you cannot do this too. This book gives you the practical steps needed to do the same in your area.

If you are not comfortable with asking friends or family for help and still do not have enough money to get started, do you give up? No way!

Have you worked out how much you spend each day on non-essential stuff in your life? If you really want to be financially free, then you have to start by being honest with yourself and work out what you can do without each month. Saving money can be a difficult habit to start, but when you know what you can achieve by investing in property over the long-term, isn't it the wisest thing to do? Cut out the non-essentials and start saving. Little by little you investment pot will grow. It just takes time.

Like the Ironman who trains for months before a race, you need to clear away all of the unnecessary financial clutter before you are ready to start your Property Ironman race. When you can afford to invest in your first property, your life changes literally overnight. You will get a huge sense of achievement, and you have begun to take financial control of your life.

So, smash down those financial hurdles now and take the first step on your Property Ironman journey.

Why Many Investors Finish Last

Regular property investors fail so often because they follow the herd and do what everyone else does. Property Ironmen are contrarian investors and they do the opposite. Here are some of the reasons why so many property investors finish last in the race:

- There's an old school of thought that says property investors need good instincts or a 'positive feeling' about a property before buying it. The problem is that instincts are not fool-proof. Don't replace research with instinct.

- Jumping on the property bandwagon and buying at market value will take you a lot longer to achieve financial freedom, if you ever get there at all. Regular investors love to tell their friends that they are 'a property investor', but only the savvy ones know they make money when they buy. Do not purchase unless you get a big discount, anything else is not investing, it is just buying. They run out of money.

- Regular property investors use all their own cash and that limits their returns and does not generate significant monthly cash flow. They expect to get rich in a few months. They have been seduced by slick salespeople offering great courses that promise a luxury lifestyle for only six easy payments of £500 per month!

- Regular property investors want the easy route to riches without putting any of the effort in. Sorry to disappoint you, but they just do not work. When they realise this, they get disgruntled and give up.

- Regular property investors do not invest in their education. They might have a little bit of property knowledge and think that will be enough, but making one simple mistake can wipe out all their savings and put them off for life. They tell anyone who will listen that property does not work, and they will look for alternatives such as stock market investing, Internet marketing, or buying gold to make 'easy' money. (*Disclaimer: you can be successful in anything if you become an expert at it!*)

- So many people want to do it alone because they think it is too expensive to pay others for their expertise. If you are 'dabbling' with property in your spare time, you are more likely to make mistakes due to your inexperience. No one can navigate the choppy waters of the property market on their own, so why bother risking it?

- They spend too much on refurbishments and make their investments a home where they would like to live, rather than thinking about what their tenants expect. Like investing in a yacht, this is a sure-fire way to spend all your money quickly without getting a return.

- They flit from one property investing strategy to another and have no focus. They start off with buying a simple buy-to-let property but before long try options, auctions, flips, HMOs, adverse possession, development, and commercial property etc. You name it, they try it – and fail at each and every one because they are distracted and don't focus on one strategy.

These are some of the reasons that so many investors finish last and never get wealthy from property investment. It really does take discipline to stick to a plan and to work a good strategy effectively. But if you do it, I promise that you will see amazing results. Don't give up; you're closer to success than you think.

Making It through a Tough Race

I do not know what your life is like right now. A tough race is always the hardest to win, but it is the most satisfying once you have completed it.

To make it through a tough race, you can't have a defeatist attitude. In Ironman, if you doubt yourself for even a moment, it's all too easy to simply stop moving and to pull out.

In property investing, if you stop pushing for the gold because it gets too hard or you get bored, I can guarantee that you will not become financially free. Both are tough races. Both will require your complete attention.

But let me tell you this, if you implement my winning 3PR framework and stick to it, I promise you that your life will change. After a while, you will experience, perhaps for the first time in your life, how it feels to NOT have to worry about money.

We all run tough races in our lives—whether they are actual races or metaphorical ones, those who have a strong motivation to succeed and persevere will win.

That's what being a Property Ironman is all about. Keep going, no matter what—overcome those obstacles, learn from your mistakes, and stay in the race.

10 Strategies for Sustainable Success

There are many ways to keep you on the right path to become a successful Property Ironman, but here are the most important ones.

1. *Be positive!* Do not let your limiting beliefs win. Trust yourself and the winning 3PR framework. You have read about those who have made it work, and you can do it too. I recommend you read Susan Jeffers's book titled, *'Feel the Fear and Do It Anyway'*.

2. *Set your property goals.* When you start, set achievable goals and celebrate when you reach them. This will spur you on to bigger goals and get you closer to your ultimate aim of financial freedom.

3. *Focus on your strategy and do not get distracted.* The 3PR framework is simple, and some would say boring! Buying, refurbishing and renting property is a sustainable strategy. Stick to it and do not get tempted by the latest, shiny property investing strategies. Remember to:

   Follow
   One
   Course
   Until
   Successful

4. *Do not wait to invest in property; invest in property and wait.* Procrastination is likely to result in you never starting! Property investing is a long-term wealth building strategy. Investing for cash flow using the 3PR framework will quickly give you a profitable income – if property prices also rise over time (as they

have always done since 1066!) then you will have an appreciating asset too. Happy days.

5. *Keep going.* When the going gets tough, and you want to give up, you must keep going. Property Ironmen do not dip in and out of property; they are dedicated to making property work. If you are persistent, you will succeed.

6. *Trust the financials and take all emotion out of the buying decision.* Sticking to your buying criteria will help you make the right investment decisions every time.

7. *Leverage.* Every investor runs out of his or her own money at some stage. Do not use this as an excuse to stop buying property! Use other people's money (bank lending or JV finance) to keep adding to your portfolio. Buying carefully with the winning 3PR framework means the returns over time are much better than tying up all your own money from the start.

8. *Only ever buy at a significant discount below the market value.* There is never a bad time to start investing in property, even when prices are rising, but you must buy at a discount to lock in your profits. Motivated sellers and repossessions (or foreclosures) are two good sources of discounted property.

9. *Property experts will save you more than they cost.* Why risk all that you have saved to invest in property because you think you can do it all yourself? Rely on the experts and their advice will pay you back ten times what they cost. The cost of my mentorship with Progressive Property a few years ago was paid back more than ten times on the first deal I bought because I got such a large discount off the market value.

10. *Mix with like-minded people.* There are many property investor communities, online forms, and networking events around, and I find they are often supportive environments for investors at all levels. Joining a local property group or creating your own is a wonderful way to reinforce your positive beliefs, cement your property knowledge, and grow your network. Any property question you have is likely to have been experienced by others in the group, so tap into this font of property knowledge. Remember that your network is your net worth.

To find out what to do next, let's now move on to the final chapter of the Property Ironman.

The Investment Triathlon Cycle

"Everyone says buying your first apartment makes you feel like an adult. What no one mentions is that selling it turns you right back into a child."

ANDERSON COOPER

Ironman events have three distinct stages—the open water swim, the long bicycle ride, and the marathon. Each is more exhausting than the next, and at times you marvel that your body is still moving, still competing. It is easy to quit at any time, but you cannot—because there is always something more challenging and rewarding around the corner. This demonstrates the persistence and determination that every Property Ironman needs, and what YOU now need to adopt to succeed.

You have the opportunity to do greater, bigger, and better things because of the money that you're making. Do not forget that it is when the serious money starts rolling in that you have the opportunity to become a millionaire.

The Starter Whistle

Right now, you have not even started training for the race. Ironman is a long event and it is going to take a lot out of you. That starter whistle is the sound of freedom. You want to get to the point where you can condition yourself enough to begin property investment the *Property Ironman* way.

It is a systematic process. You can't just decide to be an Ironman, and then sign up for the next available race. You might get as far as the second buoy in the water before someone has to fish you out from sheer exhaustion!

In the same way, you can't just suddenly become a successful *Property Ironman* investor. This book has taken you quite far into what you need to do to become one. But you have not actually done any of these steps yet. Do not get overexcited, and take that nest egg you've been saving up and blow it all on a property somewhere without really learning what I've told you.

You are at your most dangerous when you're untrained and uneducated. An Ironman that hasn't done his 'due diligence', in other words adequate technique and cardio training, is going to run out of steam, make a mistake, or get injured. The lesson rings true in property investment too.

The Property Ironman 3PR framework is really something of beauty. It is the ability to survive and thrive, event after event —and never get tired or make a wrong move. A perfectly conditioned Ironman out on that gruelling course seems right at home, like nothing in the world can stop him from winning. They feel strong and despite the challenge they enjoy every minute out there.

That is how you have to be with property investment. Nothing should be able to stop you by the time you begin. Even if you make small mistakes, you need to learn from them quickly and move on again. As you gain more experience, you will eliminate those minor errors, fine-tune your system, and quickly reach your property goals.

The starter whistle is waiting for each and every one of you. It's not easy—it may even be the hardest thing you've ever had to do, initially. But things in your life have to change, and rapid change can only do you good at this point, especially when you know what you want.

Recap: Steps 1-2

Just to make sure that you've correctly assimilated the winning 3PR framework that I used to change my life and become a property millionaire, we're going to recap it in some detail here. You can refer to these pages when you're out 'in the field' finding a deal. Learn and implement them in order.

The winning 3PR framework has three P's and three R's to create a great investment formula.

Step 1 is the first P. It involves PLACE, or where to buy your property.

Finding the right location will save you time, effort, and money. Research one area thoroughly, and find out all you can from other property experts. Consider the relative value of property and tenant demand. Find out about local amenities and transport. Always make sure that you check out the surrounding areas as comparisons.

You need to hit the streets and speak to the community, or speak to local estate agents who know the area better than you do. Find out where they would invest and where they wouldn't. You must never get emotionally involved when assessing an area; if the numbers stack up but you wouldn't want to live there yourself, so what? This is a business.

Have a location checklist of the ideal characteristics that it needs to have. If the location does not meet your criteria, then move on to somewhere else that does. Decide to invest in one location only and don't get tempted into the scattergun approach.

Remember: Find the best location to locate the best profits.

Step 2 is the second P. It involves PROPERTY, or what you must buy.

Buying the right type of property will create long-term wealth for you, so get it right from the start. Begin by researching the relative property price increases in your chosen location over time to give you an indication that your investment might grow in value in the future.

Next find out what type of housing local tenants need. When the realistic rental yield is +8.5% per annum, then you will have found the right type of property for you. If, like me, your prospective tenants are young families, then invest in two or three bed houses. Focusing on one type of property works best.

Typically, older houses were built to last, so opt for those. They also have the added bonus of a longer, proven price history compared to newly built property. If they are ugly, even better, because they will put off novice investors or first time buyers and you will get a bargain!

You must never guess what any refurbishment work will cost. So get three estimates for the work from local tradesmen and factor these costs into your analysis. You must work out the potential increase in value, and your profit, before you invest.

Research and check all your assumptions to make sure you have found the right type of property for you, but don't use it as an excuse to procrastinate. You must take action and invest if you want to be a Property Ironman!

Remember: Focus on the right property today to achieve financial freedom tomorrow.

Recap: Steps 3-4

Step 3 is the final P. It involves PRO TEAM, or building your Power Pro Team.

Every successful property investor builds a property investment team to help them. You need to leverage the expertise of others to accelerate your success and stop you making costly mistakes.

The goal of your Power Pro Team is to be a font of knowledge that you can tap into during your investment journey. They give you different perspectives, keep you on track, and move you towards your property goals.

Start recruiting your Power Pro Team. They will include a property mentor, solicitor, mortgage broker, accountant, estate agent, letting agent, and various tradesmen. You will find the best people from recommendations from experienced property investors, and I have told you where you can contact them in the chapter.

Every investor will also run out of money or mortgage finance at some stage, so you will need joint venture finance to buy more property. Using other people's money can build your portfolio quicker and give your investor great returns, so start having conversations with potential JV partners now.

Investing in property can be a lonely task, so treat your Power Pro Team well to avoid mistakes, make money, and have fun!

You must use your Power Pro Team to help you buy property at a discount before adding value to it, which is the next stage in the framework.

Remember: Let the experts work hard for you, so you do not have to work hard.

Step 4 is the first R. It involves REFURBISHMENT, or touch up tips and tricks.

Having bought the property, you now need to refurbish it. Refurbishing it the right way will increase its value, and you will have tenants lining up to live in it. If you get this step right, you will make big profits and you will build a sustainable property portfolio.

The first thing you need to do is plan the refurbishment with your refurb manager before any work starts. Agree your budget and stick to it—for every £1 spent aim to increase the value of your property by £3. Keep the refurb simple and appropriate for your future tenants.

Ensure that you comply with all landlord rules and regulations to make your property safe for your tenants—if in doubt ask your local housing officer what you need to do.

Enhance the outside space of your property to help its curb appeal and start tenant viewings, even if the inside refurbishment isn't completely finished. This could minimise the time before tenants can move in and speed up the start of your cash flow.

Remember: Control your costs to release your profits.

Recap: Steps 5-6

Step 5 is the second R. It involves RENT, or learning how to finance your lifestyle.

Now that you have refurbished your property, you need to rent it out to. Renting the *Property Ironman* way is a stress-free process, and allows you to sit back and count your rental income each and every month.

The first thing to do is to find a great letting agent who understands your business so he or she can manage your property for you. Ideally, this person will be a property investor and landlord too. He or she will advertise your property, conduct viewings, and do adequate checks on your prospective tenants before allowing them to move in.

Then you need to listen to the advice your letting agent gives you and follow it. Insure your property against damage and voids, save some of the monthly profit for unexpected repairs, and get any damage fixed quickly. Showing your tenants that you are a responsible landlord will make them more likely to look after your property and to stay longer. These simple steps will make you more profit.

Step 5 in my 3PR framework is all about building you a continuous revenue stream. It is more reliable than any sort of pension, and best of all is that rent increases every year so it grows with you.

Remember: Look after your tenants, and your tenants will look after you.

Step 6 is the final R. It involves REFINANCE, or learning how to recycle your money.

Now that you have a growing passive income from your rent, this last step is about recycling some or all of your initial investment to buy again. This is the culmination of the first five steps. Having bought your property at a discount, refurbished it to add value, and successfully rented it out, you now need to get it re-valued at its true market value.

After six months of ownership, you will need your broker to start the remortgage process of your property by booking in a surveyor to value it. You must meet the valuer in person for the valuation appraisal at your property.

Then you will need to provide him or her with a record of what you have done to the property to improve its value (photos and receipts), and have examples of properties in your area that have sold for the price you think yours is now worth. This evidence will help you achieve the valuation you need.

There are no guarantees at this stage, but following my tips will help make your case stronger and you are more likely to be able to get some or all of your initial funds out of the property to buy again. This is how you continually, progressively, and systematically buy property after property, building your wealth until you are financially free.

Remember: Present your property well and profit will be your present.

Keeping in Touch

It is easy to read a book on becoming a successful property investor, any book at all, and decide there and then that is what you will do one day. You will get around to it at some stage when you have some more money in the bank or more time to devote to making it happen. But let's face it, saying to yourself that you will do this 'one day' in reality means you won't ever do it, and the likelihood is that you will stay where you are.

As John David Mann says in *The Eighth Day of the Week*, "'Some day…' is about some vague possibility that I'm not taking seriously. 'Some day…' is not a vision of my future. 'Some day…' is a fantasy – nothing more' ".

You might agree with what I have told you in this book and been inspired by the people in it who have become successful Property Ironmen, but it sounds like a lot of hard work does not it? As I have written before, anything done for the first time appears difficult, but with time and practise you soon get the hang of it and then wonder why you worried about it in the first place!

I can vouch for my winning 3PR framework and I know many others have made it work for them too. If you really want to change your life and those of your loved ones, take action and start. Just start, one step at a time. When I started investing in property, I was terrified of making a mistake and losing all my hard-earned money, so I know how you feel.

If you are daunted by the prospect of taking that first step, I encourage you to keep in touch with me. If you have any questions about what you have read in this book or any feedback you want to give me, please get in contact.

Alternatively, if you have started your property investing journey and want to share some of your successes, then I'd love to hear from you too!

You can email me anytime at:
Jamie@thepropertyironman.com

The Final Story: Steve Evans

I want to tell you one final story about a wonderful man called Steve Evans. He is a 50-year-old UK property investor, born and bred in London.

Steve is completely blind. Thirty years ago it was quite common for blind people to be trained as piano tuners, so Steve became a self-employed piano tuner in South London. Back in 1981 when Steve had an appointment with a client, he would sit down with his father the night before with a map on the kitchen table, and they would work out the best bus routes that he would need to take from his home to where the client lived.

Steve's father wrote down instructions on which buses to take, which direction to walk to get between different bus stops and which landmarks to be aware of, while Steve recorded these instructions into his Dictaphone. Don't forget that in those days there were no mobile phones, computers or Sat Nav systems to make his life easier, so on the day Steve just had to listen to his spoken instructions from the night before.

This meant it would take him hours to reach his appointment. It also meant that he was reliant on the buses to run on time, for the bus drivers to remember to drop him off at the right bus stop, and for any strangers who offered to help to actually give him the correct directions on how to get him to the next landmark. There was quite a lot that could, and often did, go wrong!

Can you imagine trying to get across a city on foot and using multiple buses without being able to see a thing?

Although Steve often got frustrated (mainly at the public transport system!) he never missed an appointment because he knew he had a duty to his clients, and his livelihood depended on delivering a great service for them.

Like everyone else, Steve's personality and values have been shaped by his upbringing and environment, but it is his resilience to not rely on others, to keep on going despite the difficulties and to be 'contrarian' that makes him really stand out from the crowd in my opinion.

From a property point of view, Steve also has a valuable lesson for us all. After working for almost 30 years he realised that the pension that he had diligently been investing in every month since he was 19 years old, had HALVED in value in recent years! He couldn't believe it. Steve had done what successive governments have advised us all to do, which is to regularly put money aside into your pension so you can enjoy your retirement. After investing for 30 years, Steve's pension was projected to pay him a tiny amount every month that he would never be able to live off in retirement.

Being the independent-minded man that he is, Steve decided that his only option was to take control of his financial future by investing in property. After spending some money on his property education, Steve began investing like a professional and now has a portfolio valued at just under £1 million.

What is more important to Steve, though, is that his income from property is now more than he was earning from his piano tuning business, so he has effectively 'retired' early! In addition to that, he is growing his portfolio every year, providing good quality accommodation for those that need it, and wants to inspire other people.

His favourite strategy is to buy at a discount, refurbish

the property, and refinance it so he can do it again.

I recently asked Steve what his top tips were for other investors and he said this:

- *Find people to work with from the start, as it can be a lonely world out there.* You need someone who is as passionate about property as you are.
- *'Leverage, Manage, Do.'* Do not try to do everything yourself. Leverage others so you can grow and plan your business.
- *Keep a positive mindset.* He reminded me of Henry Ford's quote: "Whether you think you can, or think you can't – you're right".

I'm so grateful to have met Steve because he is a generous individual, and his example reminds me that whatever obstacle I am facing, it can be overcome. Steve, his wife Catherine, and his guide dog John deserve all their success, and I am very happy for them.

To me Steve is the perfect *Property Ironman* because he proves that with belief, tenacity, and perseverance, you can achieve whatever you want in property.

Winning against All Odds

Perhaps the final thought I want to leave you with is about winning, despite what the world may throw at you. I learned that while winning may have different meanings for all of us, it is something we all try and do in our lives.

There is nothing more difficult than doing something unfamiliar that you've never done before based on the advice you get from some book. I understand that, really I do. I read dozens of books before I started, and while each of them helped in some way, none prepared me for the reality of property investment.

Many others also warned me that if I left my successful 18-year career in advertising, I was putting my financial future, my family and my lifestyle at risk. But I did not achieve success because I was lucky. I won against all the odds, because I didn't stop until I was winning.

I learned that from my Ironman training and success. In an event like that, you only fail if you give up. Crawling across the finish line is still a successful result! I apply that line of thinking to everything I do in property investment.

I firmly believe that this is why I've managed to learn from my mistakes and become a *Property Ironman* investor. If you want to win against all the odds, then you need to adopt the same mindset. Take those risks. Do not ever admit to failure and keep going, even after you begin to see real financial returns in your bank account.

CONCLUSION

You can become a Property Ironman by following the plans and advice in this book.

They say that if you aren't paying attention, life-changing opportunities can pass you by. Don't let this opportunity go the same way.

Property investment is not that hard, and I hope I have proven that to you by now!

All you have to do is use the same framework that I, and many others like me, have used to become financially free.

By learning what I have done and adapting it for your circumstances, you will make a huge difference to your life. Not only will you make more money, you will be able to spend more time with your loved ones and have more choices in other areas of your life too.

It is easy to do nothing and just carry on with what you've always done. That's what has got you to where you are today, isn't it? It is also completely natural to doubt that you can change your old habits and travel a new path. Everyone has excuses why they can't do something new, but did Steve Evans or Simon Zutshi or Gill Alton or Julie Hogbin or Neil Larkin let that stand in their way? No, they didn't, and you mustn't either!

I have proven that becoming a Property Ironman is a very real and doable challenge.

Here's a great excerpt that I want to share with you from Don Fink's book *Be Iron Fit* that encapsulates for me what you will feel having bought your first property the 3PR way:

"One of the lessons you learn when you cross your first Ironman finish line is that it's not really a finish line. It's

just a milestone on a much greater journey. Now you know that what may at first seem impossible is not. Now you see obstacles and 'failures' for what they are: opportunities to learn and grow. Now you will choose action over inaction. You will always commit to your dreams."

Decide right now to choose action over inaction and become a Property Ironman.

Here's to your Passive Income (forever),

Jamie Madill

REFERENCES

CHAPTER 1:

Vitillo, Alex, *House Price Facts*, http://www. housepricefacts.com/quotes.php?page=10

What Goes Up Must Come Down: The History of UK Investment Property, http://www.best-investment-property-tips.com/uk-investment-property.html

McDonald, Oonagh, *The Subprime Mortgage Crisis Isn't Over – UK Taxpayers Remain Liable,* 7th June 2012, http://www.cityam.com/forum/the-subprime-mortgage-crisis-isn-t-over-uk-taxpayers-remain-liable

UK Mortgage Crisis, Monetos, http://www.monetos.co.uk/financing/mortgages/crisis/

Oxlade, Andrew, *The Mortgage Crisis of 2008,* http://www.thisismoney.co.uk/money/news/article-1616713/The-mortgage-crisis-of-2008.html

Aron, Janine, Meullbauer, John, *The Second UK Mortgage Crisis: Modeling and Forecasting Mortgage Arrears and Possessions,* http://www.fsa.gov.uk/pubs/consumer-research/muellbauer_feb10.pdf

The Downturn in Facts and Figures, http://news.bbc.co.uk/2/hi/business/7073131.stm

Johnson, Alex, *Coronation To Jubilee: How The Property Market Has Changed*, http://blogs.independent.co.uk/2012/05/29/coronation-to-jubilee-how-the-property-market-has-changed/

*Massive Change in UK Property Market Over 60 Years,
Jubilee Research Shows*, http://www.propertywire.
com/news/features/jubilee-property-changes-
uk-201206046601.html

CHAPTER 2:

Dweck, Carol, *The Right Mindset For Success*, 12 January
2012, http://blogs.hbr.org/ideacast/2012/01/the-right-
mindset-for-success.html

Wood, John, *16 Tips For Establishing The Right Mindset
For Living a Life of Personal Excellence*, http://www.
awaionline.com/2012/04/16-tips-for-establishing-the-
right-mindset/

Personal Goal Setting, Mindtools, http://www.mindtools.
com/page6.html

Donohue, Gene, *Goal Setting – Powerful Written Goals In
7 Easy Steps*, http://topachievement.com/goalsetting.html

Mead, Jonathan, *10 Ways To Use Laser Sharp Focus To Get More
Done*, http://zenhabits.net/laser-sharp-focus-get-more-done/

Dachis, Adam, *Top 10 Ways To Create a More Focused
and Productive Work Environment*, http://lifehacker.
com/5866866/top-10-ways-to-create-a-more-focused-and-
productive-work-environment

Arvind, *6 Secrets To Becoming More Persistent*, http://
www.arvinddevalia.com/blog/2010/04/28/become-more-
persistent/

Pavlina, Steve, *Self-Discipline: Persistence*, http://
www.stevepavlina.com/blog/2005/06/self-discipline-
persistence/

Importance of Teamwork, Management Study Guide, http://www.managementstudyguide.com/importance-of-team.htm

Understanding The Importance of Teamwork, http://www.brianmac.co.uk/articles/scni13a2.htm

Tom, *5 Ways To Cultivate Ambition*, http://www.anthroflex.com/5-ways-to-cultivate-ambition/

CHAPTER 3:

Quotes on Real Estate, http://www.notable-quotes.com/r/real_estate_quotes.html

Buying a Bungalow, http://www.ourproperty.co.uk/guides/buying_a_bungalow.html

Different Types of Property, Shelter, http://england.shelter.org.uk/get_advice/finding_a_place_to_live/Buying_and_selling/finding_a_place_to_buy/different_types_of_property

Types of Houses, Landlord Property Investment, http://www.propertyinvestmentproject.co.uk/blog/types-of-houses/

How To Buy a Property Off-Plan, http://www.primelocation.com/guides/buying/how-to-buy-a-property-off-plan/

Nationwide, *UK House Prices Since 1952*, www.nationwide.co.uk/hpi/.../UK_house_price_since_1952.xls

Hoak, Amy, *How To Buy…Investment Real Estate*, http://www.marketwatch.com/story/how-to-buy-investment-real-estate

Investment Properties Pros and Cons – a Money Buddy Guide, http://www.moneybuddy.com.au/home-loans/guide-investment-properties.html

Property Buying Pitfalls, http://www.londonpropertyfinders.co.uk/property-guides/property-buying-pitfalls/

CHAPTER 4:

Buffett, Warren, Investopedia, *The Dangers of Over-Diversifying Your Portfolio*, http://www.investopedia.com/articles/01/051601.asp#axzz2CUDDAq31

Your Property Investment Guide, Prudentiallocations.com, http://www.prudentiallocations.com/pdf/InvestmentPropertyGuide.pdf

Lambert, Simon, *Ten Tops For Buy-To-Let: The Essential Advice Property Investors Need To Consider*, http://www.thisismoney.co.uk/money/mortgageshome/article-1596759/Ten-tips-buy-let.html

YPO, *The 7 Property Steps To Financial Freedom*, page 1-27

Home Buying Guide: Introduction, http://www.home.co.uk/guides/buying/

The County of Caerphilly, in The Heart of Southern Wales, http://www.visitcaerphilly.com/

The A-Z of Property Pitfalls, http://www.primelocation.com/homes-news/the-a-to-z-of-property-pitfalls/

Tay, Gerald, *Top 30 Common Property Investment Mistakes*, http://www.crei-academy.com/top-30-common-property-investment-mistakes-2/

CHAPTER 5:

Jordan, Michael, Thinkexist, *Michael Jordan Quotes*, http://thinkexist.com/quotation/talent_wins_games-but_teamwork_and_intelligence/150227.html

Building Your Real Estate Investment Team – Part 7: Selecting a Property Manager, http://www.therentables.com/blog/building-your-real-estate-investment-team-part-7-selecting-a-property-manager

Opie, Melissa, *How To Build a Successful Property Investment Team*, http://www.therentables.com/blog/building-your-real-estate-investment-team-part-7-selecting-a-property-manager

Goins, Larry, *Building Your Real Estate Investment Team*, http://www.reiclub.com/articles/building-real-estate-team

5 Must Have Members of Your Real Estate Investment Team, http://www.dealmakersblog.com/real-estate-investment-team/

The 10 Biggest Mistakes Made By Property Investors, http://openwealthcreation.com.au/the-10-biggest-mistakes-made-by-property-investors/

CHAPTER 6:

Risk Quotes To Instill Courage, http://www.inspirational-quotes-motivate.com/risk_quotes.html

Refurbishments and Improvements, http://www.servicemagic.co.uk/tips-and-advice/refurbishment-improvement/

10 Home Renovation Tips – Learn From Our Experience, http://everydaytipsandthoughts.com/10-home-renovation-tips-learn-from-our-experience/

Tips When Refurbishing a House? http://forums. moneysavingexpert.com/showthread.php?t=3113962

Wallender, Lee, *The 4 Pitfalls of Home Renovation*, http:// homerenovations.about.com/od/legalsafetyissues/a/ artrenovpitfall.htm

Doing Up Houses For Profit, http://homerenovations. about.com/od/legalsafetyissues/a/artrenovpitfall.htm

Forshaw, Lyndon, *Property Auction Gold: £9,000 Profit in Just 48 Hours (or £30,000 in 8 weeks)*, http://www. ukpropertyexpert.com/blog/2009/05/property-auction-gold-9000-profit-in-just-48-hours-or-30000-in-8-weeks/

Renovation Tips and Tricks, 29 September 2008, http:// propertyinvestmentwise.com.au/renovation-tips-and-tricks/

Home Improvements and Home Renovations Tips and Tricks, http://www.spinners.com.au/tipsandtrickm.php

Boyd, Carolyn, *Top 10 Renovation Mistakes*, http://news. domain.com.au/domain/diy/top-10-renovation-mistakes-20100927-15tkh.html

25 Biggest Renovating Mistakes, http://www.hgtv.com/ home-improvement/25-biggest-renovating-mistakes/index. html

CHAPTER 7:

Woopidoo Quotations, http://www.woopidoo.com/ business_quotes/real-estate.htm

Fredman, Josh, *How Do I Prepare a House as Rental Property?* http://www.woopidoo.com/business_quotes/ real-estate.htm

How Do You Prepare Your Rental Property For Occupancy, http://www.allbusiness.com/personal-finance/investing-real-estate-investments/4086-1.html#axzz2CUO2aI1v

How To Prepare Your Property For Rent, http://www.loft-interiors.co.uk/Blog/entry/how-to-prepare-your-property-for-rent.html

Top 10 Features of a Profitable Rental Property, http://www.investopedia.com/articles/mortgages-real-estate/08/buy-rental-property.asp#axzz2CUDDAq31

Top 10 Mistakes Property Owners Make Part 2, http://www.arnoldproperty.com.au/top-10-mistakes-property-owners-make-part-2/

Top Ten Legal Mistakes That's Can Sink Your Landlord Business, http://www.nolo.com/legal-encyclopedia/top-legal-mistakes-landlords-30212.html

Dare Hall, Zoe, James Caan's Seven Golden Rules of Property Investment, http://www.telegraph.co.uk/property/3484488/James-Caans-seven-golden-rules-of-property-investment.html

CHAPTER 8:

Real Estate Quotes, Investing in Property, Woopidoo, http://www.woopidoo.com/business_quotes/real-estate.htm

Building Your Portfolio By Using The Same Deposit Again, and Again, and Again, http://www.propertygeek.net/building-your-portfolio/

Nationwide, *Remortgage Guide,* http://www.nationwide.co.uk/NR/rdonlyres/E4260994-AE50-400B-B204-BAF1C834070E/0/remortgageGuide.pdf

Simpson, Neil, Lambert, Simon, *How To Beat a Low Mortgage Valuation*, http://www.thisismoney.co.uk/money/mortgageshome/article-1694858/How-to-beat-a-low-mortgage-valuation.html

Desimone, Brendon, *How Appraisals Work,* http://www.zillow.com/blog/2011-12-15/how-appraisals-work/

McHood, Justin, *What You Need To Refinance an Investment Property,* http://www.zillow.com/blog/2011-12-15/how-appraisals-work/

Pogol, Gina, *Refinancing Investment property in Today's Market*, http://library.hsh.com/articles/refinancing/refinancing-investment-property-in-todays-market.html

Errors To Avoid When Refinancing A Rental Property, http://library.hsh.com/articles/refinancing/refinancing-investment-property-in-todays-market.html

The 7 Steps To Successfully Building a Property Portfolio, http://www.investmentpropertyfinders.com.au/doc_bin/7steps.pdf

CHAPTER 9:

Lombardi, Vince, *Winners and Winning*, QuotationsBook, http://quotationsbook.com/quote/41461/

How To Build a Property Portfolio, http://money.uk.msn.com/money-guides/mortgages/buy-to-let/how-to-build-a-property-portfolio

How To Build Your Own Real Estate Empire, http://www.firstrentalproperty.com/how-to-build-your-own-real-estate-empire/

CHAPTER 10:

Winfrey, Oprah, *Quotable Quote*, Goodreads, http://www. goodreads.com/quotes/24752-i-ve-come-to-believe-that-each-of-us-has-a

6 Tips For Successful Property Investment, http://www. mortgagechoice.com.au/media/187384/6%20tips%20 for%20successful%20property%20investment.pdf

Folger, Jean, *Ten Habits of Highly Effective Real Estate Investors*, http://www.forbes.com/2010/09/21/real-estate-investor-personal-finance-effective-habits.html

Von Deck, Tom, *Overcome Financial Stress and Attract Abundance*, http://www.deepermeditation.net/ stressadviceblog/overcome-financial-stress-and-attract-abundance-220

Evans, Pat, *How To Overcome Financial Stress and Fears*, http://www.deepermeditation.net/stressadviceblog/ overcome-financial-stress-and-attract-abundance-220

Yardney, Michael, *What 90% of Property Investors Fail To Do – And Why 10% Succeed,* http://propertyupdate.com. au/what-90-of-property-investors-fail-to-do-and-why-10-succeed/

Saunders, Kevin, *Why Residential Income Property Investors Fail,* http://www.touchstonepropertiesla.com/ why-residential-income-property-investors-fail/

Property Investing: Top Three Reasons Why Investors Fail To Build a Business, http://waytowealthpro.com/blog/ property-investing-top-three-reasons-why-investors-fail-build-business

The Essential Property Investment Strategy, The Money Centre, http://www.themoneycentre.net/strategy.pdf

List of Possible Real-Estate-Investment Strategies By John T Reed, http://www.johntreed.com/strategies.html

Implementing Responsible Property Investment Strategies, http://www.unpri.org/files/ResponsiblePropertyInvestmentToolkit.pdf

CHAPTER 11:

Real Estate Quotes, *Investing in Property,* Woopidoo, http://www.woopidoo.com/business_quotes/real-estate.htm

The Habits of Successful Property Investors, http://www.gpsnetwork.com.au/The-habits-of-successful-property-investors.asp

Real Estate Investor Success Stories, http://www.creonline.com/Success-Stories/index.html

Top 10 Criteria For Buying a High Performance Investment Property, http://www.investorsedgefinance.com/buying-investment-property

ABOUT THE AUTHOR

Jamie Madill left a successful 18-year advertising career behind him to pursue his joint passions for property and triathlon.

He has built a substantial property portfolio for himself and his family, and has competed in dozens of triathlons including Ironman-distance races.

He now spends most of his time helping others achieve their financial dreams by mentoring students and building property portfolios for clients.

For more information on Jamie,
visit www.thepropertyironman.com and
www.jamiemadill.com

Printed in Great Britain
by Amazon.co.uk, Ltd.,
Marston Gate.